FRENCH NOVELISTS OF TO-DAY

"Mysteriously and sadly, making many experiments and many mistakes as she goes, France is journeying towards a new ideal."

PAUL SABATIER.

avec mes respects confraternels

Anatole France

FRENCH NOVELISTS OF TO-DAY

BY WINIFRED (WHALE) STEPHENS
WITH PORTRAIT AND BIBLIOGRAPHIES

FIRST SERIES

Essay Index Reprint Series

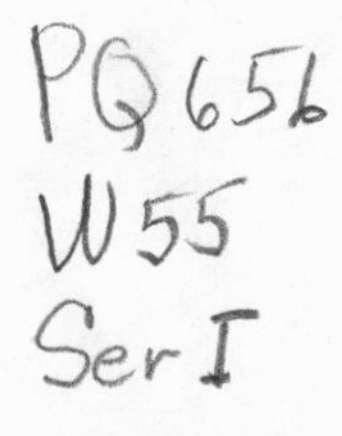

BOOKS FOR LIBRARIES PRESS
FREEPORT, NEW YORK

First Published 1914
Reprinted 1968

LIBRARY OF CONGRESS CATALOG CARD NUMBER:
68-20338
PRINTED IN THE UNITED STATES OF AMERICA

PREFACE

THE serious reader, says Sainte Beuve, resembles the pedestrian setting forth on a walking tour with his knapsack on his back. He can carry only a few articles. The difficulty is to know what to take and what to leave behind. Likewise the reader, confronted by millions of books, is perplexed as to what to read and what to leave unread. Such a selection is especially puzzling when it has to be made from a foreign literature, and one so abundant as the French; for, as every Japanese draws, so every Frenchman writes, we are told. It is the critic's business to aid the reader in his choice. To indicate what contemporary French novels are likely to interest English readers and why, is my ambition in these essays.

A veteran in the French world of letters said to me the other day, when we were discussing the subject of this book :—

"Anatole France and Maurice Barrès are

our only living novelists worth writing about." He spoke with the customary contempt of veterans for the younger generation. The present time appears dark to him as it did to Renan towards the end of his life. My friend's criticism, though somewhat severe, was just to a certain extent. He was right in assigning to France and to Barrès a pre-eminence above their contemporaries. They alone are worthy to be the successors of Balzac, Flaubert, and Maupassant, the giants of former days. Nevertheless there are others, among them Bazin, Bourget, Prévost, and Rod, whose work is full of a deep significance, while, as an artist in words, Loti is the worthy continuator of Flaubert.

The French novel is at present passing through a transition stage. A great future lies before it; but, for the moment, it lacks some great guiding impulse like the Romantic spirit of the early nineteenth century, or the Realist movement of later years. Towards the close of the last century a reaction against Realism set in; and this negative tendency is the most prominent feature of the French novel of to-day, the one bond of union between its numerous schools. Reaction against

Realism characterises alike the novel of manners of Anatole France, the sociological novel of Barrès, the psychological novel of Bourget, the passion novel of Prévost, and the moral studies of Edouard Rod. Among the writers discussed in this volume, he who is nearest the Realists is Pierre Loti, but that only in certain of his novels; his works as a whole are too ardently aglow with poetic fire to be strictly realistic; they suggest rather the romantic imagination of a Chateaubriand than the scientific observation of a Balzac.

For centuries France has been in the vanguard of European thought; and now, as formerly, her intellectual life is a seething ferment of ideas. She jeers at England for being the country of multitudinous sects; but England may justly rally France as the land of innumerable isms. These manifold currents of French thought circulate freely through the pages of the novel. Every theory finds an advocate in some contemporary novelist: socialism in Anatole France; nationalism in Maurice Barrès; clericalism in Bourget; provincialism in Bazin; femininism in Prévost, while the claims of various isms are impartially discussed in the pages of Edouard Rod.

There are those who tell us that the French novel is dead. To such we would reply: then France herself must be dead. For the novel is now the strongest and most complete expression of the French genius. No literary form in any country is so faithful a reflection of the spirit and life of the people of that country as the French novel. It is no accidental fruit of the chances of the passing hour, but an art, the roots of which strike deep into the literary traditions of the country. In judging it, therefore, we must keep ever before us the character and the history of the French people. English readers too often find immoral, gross, or indecent the very best French fiction, because they expect a Celtic-Latin race, like the French, to judge life according to Teutonic standards. Yet racial differences between English and French will deter no sensible Englishman from travelling in France, and they should not deter him from reading French novels.

"Every age must write its own books," says Emerson: and there are books for all ages; the French novel is not for the young. As one of its writers has said: "It is the fruit of maturity addressed to maturity. It represents life in its most characteristic episodes. It addresses itself to readers whom it has no idea of forming, and who should be able to bear what it has to show them as they would the scenes of actual life."

The French novelist's treatment of love would alone render his books unsuitable for "the young person." But it must be remembered that in French society marriage is a mere social contract, not necessarily involving love; love in French novels is therefore usually outside the marital relations.

French writers hold various views as to the object of the novel. On the whole, the novel with a purpose has a greater vogue in France than in England. One generally finds a novelist at the outset of his career espousing Flaubert's doctrine of "art for art's sake." Then, like our own George Eliot, as he advances in a knowledge of life and its conditions, he grows more and more lenient towards the novel with a purpose, and almost invariably ends by writing it. Even such a complete personification of the artistic temperament as Pierre Loti has in these last days yielded something to the attractions of the more actual form of fiction; in his latest novel, *Les Désenchantées*, behind the impressions of life in

Turkish harems, a moral purpose is clearly discernible: the book is intended to demonstrate the evil of an attempt to graft western culture on oriental institutions.

Ever since the days of Voltaire, French prose has been one of the most perfect mediums for the expression of human thought. The traditions of this fine art are to-day worthily maintained in the pages of the novel, by the finely finished rhythmic sentences of Anatole France, the harmonious phrases of Barrès, the simple exactitude of Loti's vivid word pictures.

As psychologists all these writers excel. With unerring hand they probe the mysteries of the human heart. With each one we inevitably associate some type of humanity immortalised in his works: with France the scholar, with Barrès the politician, with Bazin the peasant, with Loti the sailor, with Rod the lover, with Bourget the fashionable cynic, with Prévost woman in her various phases.

To this gallery of portraits have been added those national types outlined in the four novels of Pierre de Coulevain. In her striking contrasts between the French temperament and that of English and Americans, this writer brings into high relief those essential elements of the French genius which lie at the heart of the French novel.

The bibliographies include other works besides novels; but, to avoid confusion, the titles of works of fiction will be found printed in larger type.

The writer wishes to thank those of the authors discussed in the volume, and others, who have rendered her kindly aid in the compilation of these bibliographical lists.

She would also acknowledge her indebtedness to Monsieur Pierre Champion of Paris, who has read the essay on Anatole France.

LONDON, 1908.

CONTENTS

ANATOLE FRANCE

THE WORKS OF ANATOLE FRANCE

1859. La Légende de Sainte Radegonde, reine de France. (Only a small number produced in facsimile from the original manuscript.)
1868. Alfred de Vigny.
1873. Les Poèmes Dorés.
1875. Bernardin de Saint Pierre et la Princesse Marie Miesnik. } (Extr. de L'Amateur d'Autographes.)
Les Poèmes de Jules Breton.
Racine et Nicole—La Querelle des Imaginaires.
1876. Les Noces Corinthiennes.
1879. Lucile de Chateaubriand.
Jocaste et le Chat Maigre.
1881. **Le Crime de Sylvestre Bonnard.**
1882. **Les Désirs de Jean Servien.**
1885. **Le Livre de Mon Ami.**
1886. **Nos Enfants, Scènes de la Ville et des Champs.** (A children's book, illustrated by M. Boutet de Monvel.)
1888. La Vie Littéraire.
1889. ,, ,, (Second series.)
Balthasar.
1890. **Thaïs.**
1891. Notice Historique sur Vivant Denon (afterwards incorporated in La Vie Littéraire).
La Vie Littéraire. (Third series.)
1892. La Vie Littéraire. (Fourth series.)
L'Étui de Nacre.
1893. L'Elvire de Lamartine. Notes sur Monsieur et Madame Charles.
La Rôtisserie de la Reine Pédauque.
Les Opinions de Monsieur Jérôme Coignard.
1894. **Le Lys Rouge.**
La Société Historique d'Auteuil et de Passy. (Lecture.)
1895. **Le Jardin d'Épicure.**
Le Puits de Sainte Claire.
1896. Collected Poems. (Les Poèmes Dorés, Idylles et Légendes, Noces Corinthiennes.)
1897. Discours de Réception à l'Académie Française.
L'Orme du Mail.
Le Mannequin d'Osier.
1898. Au Petit Bonheur. (Comedy in one Act.)
1899. Etienne Charavay, 1848-1899. (Speech.)
L'Anneau d'Améthyste.
Pierre Nozière.

1900. **Clio.**
Filles et Garçons. (A reprint, with the corresponding illustrations, of ten of the children's stories in **Nos Enfants.**)

1901. **Monsieur Bergeret à Paris.**
L'Affaire Crainquebille.
Cahiers de la Quinzaine. (La Liberté par l'Etude. La Loi est Morte mais le juge est vivant. Vol domestique. Les juges intègres.)

1902. Funérailles d'Emile Zola. (Oration.)
Opinions Sociales.

1903. **Histoire Comique.**
Discours Prononcé à l'Inauguration de la Statue d'Ernest Renan à Tréguier.
Sur la Tombe de Pierre Laffitte. (Oration.)

1904. **Crainquebille, Putois, Riquet et Plusieurs autres Récits profitables.**
L'Eglise et la République.

1905. **Sur la Pierre Blanche.**

1906. Vers les Temps Meilleurs. (Volume of Speeches.)

1908. Vie de Jeanne d'Arc.
In course of publication—
Les Contes de Jacques Tournebroche.
Les Pingouins.

Abeille, one of the stories afterwards incorporated in the volume entitled *Balthasar*, appeared in 1883, as a children's book, with coloured illustrations by Carl Gehrts.

From *L'Étui de Nacre* three stories were afterwards selected for separate publication in 1902. *Mme. de Luzy*, with illustrations by A. Lalauze; *Mémoires d'un Volontaire*, with illustrations by A. Moreau; and *Le Procurateur de Judée*, with illustrations by A. F. Gorguet.

Editions were issued in 1900 of *Thaïs*, with illustrations by P. A. Laurens; and of *Clio*, with illustrations by Mucha—no unillustrated edition of this volume has yet appeared; and of *Histoire Comique*, with illustrations by E. Chahine, in 1903.

An edition of *L'Affaire Crainquebille* (the story), with illustrations by Steinlen, appeared in 1901. And in 1902 the *Funérailles d'Emile Zola* also was illustrated by Steinlen.

An edition of *Les Noces Corinthiennes*, with illustrations by A. Leroux, has also appeared.

Les Contes de Jacques Tournebroche will include *La Leçon bien apprise*, issued privately in 1898, with illustrations by L. Lebègue, and *Le Traitté des phantosmes de Nicole Langelier*, renamed *De Une Horrible Paincture*, which appeared privately with a paper on *Jean Gutenberg* (republished in *Vers les Temps Meilleurs*), with illustrations by Steinlen, Bellery-Desfontaines, G. Bellenger, and F. Florian, in 1900.

ANATOLE FRANCE, 1844

"In peace of mind, therefore, let us leave the planet to accomplish her destiny. Our outcries will be useless; our ill-humour will be out of place. It is possible that the Earth may fail to achieve her object, as must probably have already happened in innumerable other worlds. It may even be that our time will be one day considered as the culminating point after which humanity declined. But the universe knows no discouragement; it is always recommencing its abortive work. Each failure leaves it young, alert, full of illusions. . . . When one can make mistakes with impunity, one is sure of succeeding in the end. Happy those who collaborate in the great final success, the complete coming of God."—RENAN.

JACQUES ANATOLE THIBAULT, who was to write under the name of *France*, was born in Paris on April 16, 1844. It was an appropriate coincidence that he, whose originality of thought and courage in its expression was so forcibly to recall Voltaire, should have first seen the light in a house only a few doors away from where the apostle of Ferney died. As one crosses the Seine from the right to the left bank, over Le Pont Carrousel, there is a shop almost immediately facing the bridge, No. 9 Quai Voltaire, where in the year 1844 Monsieur Thibault, then a well-known bookseller, himself also a writer and a great authority on eighteenth century history, carried on his business. In an *appartement* giving on the *cour* behind the shop, Monsieur Thibault's son, Anatole, was born. The *nom de guerre* of France, which Anatole was to render so familiar throughout the cultured world, he inherited from his father. Thibault the elder received it from his comrades when he was doing military service. It stuck to him throughout life, and he handed it on to his son.

The shop of France the elder, the French Dodsley of the middle of the last century, was the rendezvous of the greatest writers of the day. Now, alas! it has fallen to base uses. As I write, there comes a letter from a friend in Paris telling how *la pauvre boutique du Père France* is *bien somptueusement transformée.* The house has been bought by a furniture dealer. "And now, where the shop once stood," writes my friend, "there is being erected a monumental staircase. This shop was a relic of those scholars and writers from all parts of the world who entered it in quest of some rare book or valuable piece of information. Oh, the sadness of departing things!"

Anatole, as a schoolboy, lingering behind his father's counter, and later as a budding bookseller sitting at his desk, must have listened to many a discussion afterwards re-echoed in the conversations of l'Abbé Jérôme Coignard and his friends at *l'Image de Sainte Catherine* or of Monsieur Bergeret, *chez Paillot*, *Libraire.* While from his father Anatole inherited a passion for the doctrines of the Revolution, his mother early instilled into his mind an interest in the religion of his country. He was brought up on the *Lives of the Saints.* He read them at his mother's knee, and the love of those quaint old stories has never left him. Their influence is to be seen in many of his works; and how the stories of saints and martyrs moulded his child life he has told in one of the most delightful of his books, *Le Livre de Mon Ami.* "At seven years old I did not know how to read; I wore divided skirts; I cried when my nurse wiped my nose, and I was devoured by ambition," he writes. "If I had been able I would have gone forth to win immortality on the battlefield; but a horse, a uniform, a regiment, enemies, were not for me. Therefore I thought of becoming a saint. The profession of saint has fewer requirements and wins greater renown than that of a soldier."

His youthful strivings after sainthood, however, were destined to meet with misconstruction from the members of his household. Fasting, by refusing his breakfast, made his mother think he must be ill. When, following the example of St. Simon, the blessed hermit of the column, he climbed the kitchen pump, Julie, the servant, said he could not live there, and lifted him down. He received no encouragement from his father when, emulating the generosity of St. Nicholas of Patras, he threw out of the study window his playthings and twelve precious new sous. His father, shutting the window, exclaimed, "The boy must be mad;" but then, his father was no saint and therefore could not understand. From his mother he might have expected sympathy, but even she was so dull of comprehension as to be really distressed when, starting for his walk, this young aspirant to sainthood tore the feather out of his hat in imitation of the holy St. Labre, who never put on his cap without previously dragging it in the mud. Neither did his attempt to manufacture for himself a hair-shirt out of one of the cushions of the dining-room chairs meet with any more charitable appreciation; it only gained for him a sound whipping, and so he was put to bed, having been driven to the conclusion that it is hard to practise sainthood in the bosom of one's family. Thus he came to understand why St. Anthony and St. Jerome had been compelled to renounce all intercourse with their fellows and live in a desert among savage beasts; indeed he himself had serious thoughts of retiring to "Le Jardin des Plantes" to take up his abode among the wild animals there.

The school he attended was the Collège Stanislas; but his real education, he tells in *Le Livre de Mon Ami* and *Pierre Nozière*, was derived from promiscuous reading, wanderings along the old quays of Paris, loiterings in the streets. There, by watching the milkmen, the coal-heavers, and the water-carriers coming round in the morning, and the soldiers marching to the music of their band, and by peering into the wine shops and the grocers' stores, he learnt better than anywhere else the working of that great social machine which assigns to every one his task in the world.

While he derived his practical education from the sights and sounds of the streets, his book-learning he owed not so much to the university professors as to the old Jewish dealers of curiosity shops and to the keepers of second-hand bookstalls on the quays.

"Good people," he writes, "what gratitude I owe you. . . . You displayed before my ravished gaze the mysterious form of the life of the past and all kinds of precious monuments of human thought. Searching through your boxes, looking over your dusty shelves, laden with the poor relics of our fathers and their great thoughts, all unconsciously I imbibed the most healthy philosophy."

As we should suspect Anatole was too much of a loafer to be a model pupil; his schoolmasters accused him of laziness, and he gained no high distinctions in his class. He was too original to follow blindly and industriously the regular school curriculum. In these days of discussion as to the relative merits of a classical and a scientific education it is interesting to note what our author has to say on the subject.

"I believe," he writes in *Le Livre de Mon Ami*, "that in the forming of a man's mind nothing can equal the study of the two antiquities according to the methods of the old French humanists," not, we observe, according to the methods of an English public school. "I then had a taste for good Latin and good French, which I have not yet lost, in spite of the counsels and the examples of my most successful contemporaries. There has happened to me what generally happens to people whose beliefs are scorned. I have become proud of what may be only ridiculous. I have persevered in my literary studies, and I have remained a classicist. At the risk of being regarded as an aristocrat and a mandarin, I believe that six or seven years of literary culture impart to the mind well prepared to receive it a nobility, a strength, and a beauty which can be obtained by no other means."

Nowadays when the merits of a literary education are too often underrated, and physical science bestrides us like a Colossus, it is well to find one of the most original of modern thinkers, and perhaps the greatest living master of style, opposing the views of Herbert Spencer and his school, and championing the cause of humanism in education. Fortunately for the world, or rather, for that part of it which can enjoy literature as a fine art, our author has remained a classicist. His phrase has all the clearness, the conciseness, and the delicately moulded form of the best Latin prose.

It was as a critic that Anatole made his début in literature. His first published work, which appeared in 1868, was a critical and biographical study of Alfred de Vigny. The success of this book procured for him five years later from Monsieur Lemerre the commission to edit a series of French classics. With what wide knowledge of French literature and discriminating criticism this work was carried out, the editions of Margaret of Angoulême's *Heptaméron* and Madame de la Fayette's *Princesse de Clèves* abundantly testify. At this time also he was engaged in journalism, writing for several periodicals, and contributing to *Le Temps* those brilliant articles of literary criticism published later in the volumes of *La Vie Littéraire*. In truth he is one of the greatest of living literary critics. Students of French literature can choose no surer guide. Himself a master of style, he is an unerring judge of the style of others. One of the keenest psychologists, his insight into human nature is never at fault. He has the power, not so uncommon in France as it is in England, of summing up a writer or a book in one short phrase or sentence which lives in the memory. Sainte-Beuve he calls "the Thomas Aquinas of the nineteenth century." In *Le Lys Rouge* he compares Rabelais' *Pantagruel* to "a fine and beautiful town, full of palaces, splendid in the dawn, notwithstanding that the sweepers have yet to arrive to remove the filth and the servants to wash the marble pavements." During these years he was also trying his hand at poetry; he published two volumes of verse, one entitled *Les Poèmes Dorés* in 1873, another *Les Noces Corinthiennes* in 1876. In this year he was appointed Librarian to the Senate. But these were not years of any continuous literary activity. At this time he was seeking his vocation. The desultory habits that in his boyhood caused him to loiter in the streets round second-hand bookstalls and in the old curiosity shops, were now carrying his intellectual curiosity into neglected byways of history and literature, both ancient and modern. Such habits, which would spell ruin for a mind less keen and vigorous than that of our author, were in his case developing his intelligence and storing his mind with that treasure of rare erudition which, vivified by the sparkling rays of his genius, was to prove one of the greatest charms of his writings.

In 1881, his 'prentice period ended; for it was in this year that appeared his first novel of mark, *Le Crime de Sylvestre Bonnard.* At once it became evident that the writer had at last discovered his vocation. Unlike many authors, the genius of Anatole France, as we may now call him, was speedily recognised. The novel was crowned by the French Academy, which later was to admit the writer within its ranks. *Le Crime de Sylvestre Bonnard* is one of the few of his works that have been translated into English. Both in the English and French versions it is in England the most widely read of all his novels. And indeed readers unacquainted with his works and desirous of studying them cannot make a better beginning than with *Le Crime de Sylvestre Bonnard.* The book possesses the distinctive features of his writing, that clear, forcible, and classical style, that concentration of interest not so much on the plot as on the portrayal of character, revealed not in the action but in the conversation of the personages. It has been said that Scott describes his characters from the outside to the in, and Shakespeare from the inside to the out. In this respect Anatole France resembles Shakespeare. Some writers find it necessary to explain their personages, to discourse on them as a street hawker does on his wares. Monsieur France adopts the more difficult dramatic method of making them explain themselves in conversation. His heroes and heroines are always conversing, on all manner of subjects public and private, ancient and modern, sacred and profane, and in all manner of places, at dinner parties, funerals, over shop counters, under the elm-tree of *L'Histoire Contemporaine*, in the bakehouse of *La Reine Pédauque*, in the African desert of *Thaïs*, and among the excavations of the Forum in *Sur la Pierre Blanche*. When his characters are unable to converse through the absence of a companion, or, like the dog Riquet, through lacking the faculty of human speech, then he sets them to reflect audibly ; and their reflections are as illuminating as their conversations. In several volumes, notably *Le Jardin d'Épicure* and *Sur la Pierre Blanche*, Monsieur France permits himself to reflect in his own person for the benefit and entertainment of his readers.

"Every novel," he says elsewhere, "if regarded from the right point of view, is an autobiography;" and it is not difficult to discover in his own novels, characters which are more especially the expression of the writer's own personality—Monsieur Bergeret, Jérôme Coignard, and Sylvestre Bonnard.

Bonnard has much in common with all these characters. Like the good abbé, Monsieur Coignard, like the Bohemian Choulette, like the hero of *L'Histoire Contemporaine*, Bonnard is a scholar who finds his greatest joy in books; but he is no bookworm, no mere Dryasdust; he retains in his nature much of the "milk of human kindness," his love of books has not extinguished his love of his fellow creatures. Nevertheless, living in the seclusion of his library, he has got a little out of touch with actuality; he has become obtuse on some points of practical everyday life. Well acquainted with the laws of his country from the reign of Clovis down to the sixteenth century, of more recent legislation he is totally ignorant. He therefore does not realise that he is committing a serious legal offence when, for the sake of her dead mother, he carries away from her unhappiness at school, a young girl in whom he is deeply interested. Up to a certain point the story recalls Mr. Hardy's *Well Beloved*, but in Monsieur France's novel the *dénoûment* is different. Bonnard does not allow himself to fall in love with his ward. His affection for her is paternal; and in the end she marries a man of her own age.

The appearance of "Sylvestre Bonnard" marked a turning-point in Monsieur France's career. He now became a comparatively prolific writer. *Les Désirs de Jean Servien*, *Le Livre de Mon Ami*, *L'Étui de Nacre*, and *Balthasar*, works varying greatly in merit, appeared in quick succession. In the two last, both volumes of short stories, the author revealed himself as a master of that *nouvelle* which, from the Middle Ages downwards, has been typical of French literature.

His genius has never attained a higher expression than in *Balthasar*, the story of an Ethiopian king, who travelled to a far country to make a commercial treaty with Balkis, Queen of Sheba. Overcome by her beauty, the Ethiopian becomes her willing slave. To satisfy her wild caprice, he wanders with her in disguise through the streets of the city by night. While defending her from the insults of brigands, he is wounded and lies for days raging in delirium. When, having returned to his right mind, he speaks to the Queen of their love, she appears to have forgotten it, and accuses him of having been drunk with palm wine.

Disconsolate and despairing Balthasar returns to Ethiopia. There he finds comfort in the study of astronomy. He builds a high tower whence he discovers a new star. Balkis, hearing that astrology has taken her place in the King's affection, is seized with jealousy. She makes an effort to rekindle his love for her. She journeys to the foot of the tower. Regarding her from above, Balthasar wavers for a moment. Then the Star speaks to him, saying: "Glory to God in the highest, and on earth peace, goodwill toward men. Take a measure of myrrh, gentle King Balthasar, and follow me. I will lead thee to the feet of a little child, who has just been born in a stable, by the side of an ox and an ass.

"And this little child is the King of kings. He will comfort those who wish to be comforted. Thou, Balthasar, whose soul is as dark as thy countenance, but whose heart is as simple as a child's, He calls thee to Him. He has chosen thee because thou hast suffered. He will give thee riches, joy, and love.

"He will say unto thee: Be poor with gladness; for thus only shalt thou be truly rich; true joy consists in renouncing joy. Love Me and only love My creatures in Me, for I alone am love."

As he listened to these words a divine peace was shed abroad in the King's soul; his dusky countenance became radiant; he felt himself a new man. And Balkis, as she contemplated him from below, saw that the divine love had banished her for ever from his heart. Pale with indignation she turned her back on the Ethiopian king and his kingdom and returned to her own land.

Balthasar, obedient to the Star's behest, followed it where it led him towards the west. On the way he fell in with two other kings following the. same heavenly guide. They came to Bethlehem of Judæa; and there they entered into a house and found the child, with Mary His mother; and they fell down and worshipped Him; and when they opened their treasures, they presented unto Him gifts, gold and frankincense and myrrh.

In this story we have a foretaste of those powers which, in the author's later works, were to prove his strongest attractions: delicate irony, subtle humour, and keen insight into character. It shows that strong feeling for Christian lore which had resulted from his mother's early training. But here as always, in the treatment of no matter what subject, his point of view is essentially original. The earlier part of the story is pervaded by that Gallic spirit, almost Rabelaisian in its freedom, certainly not saintly, which inevitably shocks many English readers. Still, as must appear from the foregoing summary, the biblical narrative is here treated with a reverence which it is not easy to find in some of Monsieur France's later works. The style of *Balthasar*, clear, polished, concise, forcible, is Anatole France at his best. With a masterly hand he wields that short sentence, in which, ever since the days of Voltaire, the great power of French prose has resided. There are other stories in the same volume; but *Balthasar* is by far the most powerful. The book appeared in 1889.

In 1890 came another masterpiece, *Thaïs*, one of the author's greatest productions. This novel was the first of his works to give an adequate idea of his immense erudition, embracing patristic writings as well as classical literature. Its descriptions of the Egyptian desert and the banks of the Nile prove that it may be possible for an author to represent perfectly accurate local colour without ever having visited the country. The story is the terrible tragedy of a soul at the very gate of heaven, hurled down to hell, not through any failing of his own, but through his attempt to rescue from degradation the soul of another. Under the influence of Paphnutius the hermit, Thaïs, the talented actress and beautiful courtesan, abandons her sinful life, becomes a nun, and dies the death of a saint. For, in his desert solitude, it has been borne in upon Paphnutius that he is to save the soul of Thaïs. He quits his retreat and travels to Alexandria, where he persuades Thaïs to renounce the world and lead a religious life. He conducts his penitent to a convent and there leaves her to return to the desert. But from that moment devils assail his soul. To escape the temptations with which they torture him, he abandons his hermit's hut and flees from place to place, now to the top of a column, now to a place of tombs, but all without avail ; his persecutors follow him wherever he goes, and, in the last chapter, accursed and hideous, in degradation and despair, he turns away from the saintly death-bed of his convert.

As the arena of this soul drama, the writer represents, on the one hand, the ascetic life of early Christian hermits in the African desert, and on the other the oriental Sybaritism of Alexandria and the various currents of thought in the Roman world of the first decade of the fourth century. The latter are powerfully set forth in the famous banquet scene in the house of Nicias, a Roman philosopher at Alexandria. *Thaïs* is not milk for babes. It is strong meat. To some serious readers it will be a stumbling-block. To some ignorant readers it will be foolishness. Yet in truth its satire so piercing, its humour so subtle, its irony so delicate, raise it to the first rank in fiction of high and serious import.

In a much lighter vein, though still with an eye on central and eternal questions, are two novels that appeared in 1893, three years after *Thaïs*. These were *La Rôtisserie de la Reine Pédauque*, and its companion volume, *Les*

Opinions de Monsieur Jérôme Coignard. In the earlier novel the plot is involved and fantastic, in the later, which is a kind of commentary on its predecessor, the plot vanishes altogether. Both novels are rich with fine character delineation and delicious humour. In both the scene is laid in eighteenth century France, and the spirit of the age is vividly reproduced. The machinery of sylphs and salamanders in *La Rôtisserie de la Reine Pédauque* recalls *The Rape of the Lock.* The hero of these two volumes, Monsieur Jérôme Coignard, one of those scholarly Bohemians Monsieur France excels in depicting, is one of his finest creations.

Monsieur Coignard is an abbé, once librarian to the Bishop of Séez, but now fallen from that dignified office to the more humble one of scrivener in the cemetery of the Innocents at Paris.

This monotonous calling does not depress the good abbé's natural gaiety or damp the salt of his Gallic wit. Like his successor, Monsieur Bergeret, l'Abbé Coignard is a true philosopher who bears without a murmur many a hard blow from Dame Fortune's wheel. *Bon viveur*, joyful companion, devout Catholic, profound scholar, he is a strange mixture of Epicurus and St. Francis of Assisi. His work, apparently as light as his income was meagre, permitted him to linger at will in his favourite haunts in the Rue St. Jacques, the most Bohemian quarter of eighteenth century Paris. Here at some time of the day one might be sure of finding Monsieur Coignard in threadbare cassock, spending his last *sou* in the tavern, Le Petit Bacchus, turning over the leaves of a new book fresh from Holland in the shop of Monsieur Blaizot, discussing philosophy with his pupil Jack Turnspit in the porch of St. Bénoit le Bétourné, or chatting merrily to that pupil's father, the master of the bakehouse, La Rôtisserie de la Reine Pédauque, which gives its name to the book. Later in the story, Monsieur Coignard with the Turnspit is translated from the Innocents' Cemetery to a library, not this time the library of a bishop but that of a certain mysterious Monsieur d'Astarac, an alchemist who believes in the existence of salamanders and holds converse with sylphs. In Monsieur d'Astarac's library, a long gallery, lighted by six high windows, inhabited by "an innumerable army or rather a vast council of books," the abbé and the ex-turnspit spend delightful hours. Monsieur France is himself a bibliophile and the possessor of a fine collection of rare editions and beautifully bound volumes. The very thought of a library always fires his imagination, no matter whether it be Monsieur Bergeret's plain and bare little study, with its rows of deal shelves, or the Duc de Brécé's stately hall with its statues and locked book-cases, or the book-room of an Alexandrian philosopher with seats of ivory and hundreds of papyrus rolls. But the good abbé does not long remain with Monsieur d'Astarac, his Bohemianism cannot long be kept under. Fleeing with the turnspit and other companions from the consequences of a midnight adventure, he falls a victim to the vengeance of an aged and angry Jew, and passes away, with his last breath giving wise counsel to his pupil. Jack Turnspit commemorates his master's virtues in an elegant Latin epitaph and in these two volumes, *La Rôtisserie de la Reine Pédauque* and *Les Opinions de Monsieur Jérôme Coignard*, which however he did not publish. It remained, so we are told, for Monsieur France, a century later, to discover them in the window of a curiosity shop amidst a heap of crosses and old medals.

Next to Monsieur Coignard himself, the most fascinating character of these volumes is the turnspit's mother, the baker's wife, Barbe, "good and saintly Barbe," *une digne et sainte femme*, as her husband used to call her, when he returned from the tavern late at night. "Barbe, sleep in peace," he would say; "as I was remarking just now to the lame knife-grinder, you are a good and holy woman." Barbe's oracle was the priest. M. le Curé's opinion on all manner of topics was invariably introduced into those interminable discussions which went on every day in the bakehouse. "One may doubt the evidence of one's own eyesight," she used to say, "but never the word of an honest man, especially when he belongs to the Church." On *les jours maigres* Barbe insisted on every occupant of the house, even the dog, Miraut, joining in the fast. It was in vain that her husband protested that as Miraut enjoyed none of the benefits of Christianity he ought not to be subject to its penances; but Barbe maintained that "if he had his bone as usual, and so did not fast, she would hate him as if he were a Jew." To such a literal mind as Barbe's figures of speech were incomprehensible. When the abbé offers to make a scholar of her son, invoking in classic phrase "the bees of Mount Hymettus to settle in harmonious swarms on the lips of Jack Turnspit, henceforth sacred to the muse," Barbe vehemently repudiates the honour. She remembers only too well, she says, the agony she endured when a single member of the classic swarm deigned to alight on her person. She covets no such painful privilege for her son. When Jack Turnspit goes to work in Monsieur d'Astarac's library, his mother hearing that the alchemist is a heretic and a sorcerer, is filled with misgivings, which completely vanish when Jack assures her that he is working in Greek, the language of the Bible.

English readers will be specially interested in one of the customers of the bakehouse, Mr. Shippen, an English locksmith from Greenwich. Mr. Shippen, puffed up with national pride in the English constitution, English freedom, and the English Parliament, is shocked to find that the announcement of a change in the English ministry is regarded as an event of no importance by his French acquaintances.

"Everything that happens in England is important," he cries, and departs without even wishing them good evening.

During the three years 1894, 1895, 1896, Monsieur France produced three works, styled novels, *Le Lys Rouge*, *Le Puits de Sainte Claire*, and *Le Jardin d'Épicure*. *Le Lys Rouge* stands apart. It has a clearly defined plot and is a novel of fashionable society. The scene, when, as in the greater part of the work, it is laid in Florence, is depicted with an artistic touch of Florentine colour. A striking group of dilettanti and virtuosi is described somewhat in the Meredithean manner. But, as they move across the stage they become profoundly interesting, for they give Monsieur France opportunities to reveal that philosophy of life which is the charm of the intellectual background of all his work. This novel contains a masterly creation, the character of Choulette, another scholarly Bohemian, this time of the type of Paul Verlaine, with whom the author had collaborated in his journalist days.

Le Puits de Sainte Claire, introduced by a

preface, which is a gem of his most classic style, is one of his most fantastic works. Like *Thaïs*, it reveals his intimate acquaintance with patristic lore. *Le Jardin d'Épicure*, a series of reflections profound and suggestive, unconnected by the slightest thread of plot, cannot claim to be considered as a novel.

These two volumes sink into comparative insignificance when we turn to the series entitled *L'Histoire Contemporaine*, which appeared between 1897 and 1900. The four volumes of this series, *L'Orme du Mail*, *Le Mannequin d'Osier*, *L'Anneau d'Améthyste*, and *Monsieur Bergeret à Paris*, contain some of the author's finest work in social and political criticism.

In all four the hero is nominally Monsieur Bergeret, who must surely be Monsieur France himself. In his preface to *La Vie Littéraire* he had described himself as a philosopher monk, at heart belonging to "an abbey of Thelema, in which the rule is light and obedience easy. If the faith of its inhabitants is not very strong, they are at any rate very pious." Just such a character is Monsieur Bergeret, *maître de conférences* at the University of the provincial town of ——. He makes his first appearance in Chapter VII. of *L'Orme du Mail.* Seated on a bench of the Mall, beneath the elm which gives its name to the book, Monsieur Bergeret is conversing with the Abbé Lantaigne, the superintendent of the Catholic Seminary. M. Bergeret and the Abbé hold different opinions on every subject; but they alone in that town are interested in general ideas; and this is the bond which brings them together on fine summer evenings to philosophise in the elm tree's shade and to console each other, one for the loneliness of celibacy, the other for the worries of family life. Monsieur Bergeret is poor; his house is small and uncomfortable; Madame Bergeret has a vulgar soul and his daughters do not love him. In his own house he is always being hunted from room to room for weighty domestic reasons, and he cannot call even his little study his own. All manner of feminine muddles encumber his writing-table, on which the Mesdemoiselles Bergeret make out their washing lists, draw up their accounts, and try their curling irons on his manuscripts. In front of the book-shelves that contain his learned editions of Catullus and Petronius, Madame Bergeret insists on keeping that implement of wickerwork so necessary to home dressmakers, known in France as "un mannequin d'osier," and in certain English circles termed an *angelina*. Whenever Monsieur Bergeret wishes to consult his favourite Latin authors, he must needs embrace the unyielding form of *angelina* and remove that image of conjugal felicity. At home Monsieur Bergeret's lot is plainly not a happy one, and at the University it is not much better; for there the Latin studies that he professes are under a cloud; and, while spacious halls and up-to-date laboratories are provided for the teaching of science, Monsieur Bergeret is condemned to conduct his classes in a dark, damp, unventilated room, whither only a very small number of pupils can be induced to follow him. Nevertheless, persecuted as he is at home and abroad, in his more philosophic moments Monsieur Bergeret persuades himself that he is unfortunate through his own fault. "For," like some stoic of old, he tells himself, "all our miseries proceed from within and are caused by ourselves. We believe, erroneously, that they come from without. We form them within us, out of our own substance."

Madame Bergeret's *Mannequin d'Osier* gives

its name to the second volume of *L'Histoire Contemporaine*. This volume relates a domestic crisis, which results in the inevitable separation of Monsieur and Madame Bergeret. Madame Bergeret returns to her mother's home, accompanied by her two younger daughters, while the eldest, Pauline, is to remain with her father; but for the moment Pauline is away, staying with her aunt Zoë, Monsieur Bergeret's sister. So Monsieur Bergeret, in his new lodging, is left alone with an old servant, Angélique, who takes pity on her master's friendlessness and provides him with a companion. In *L'Anneau d'Améthyste* we are told how Monsieur Bergeret, sitting in his study one morning, hears a knocking at the door. Angélique comes in, bearing in her apron a little mongrel dog: "*un petit chien de race incertaine.*" The cunning with which the old servant elicits Monsieur Bergeret's interest in the puppy is delightfully portrayed. The dog, which Angélique has instinctively named Riquet, is to become as famous a character in the novels of Monsieur France as Monsieur Bergeret himself. *Monsieur Bergeret à Paris*, the last volume of *L'Histoire Contemporaine*, is full of Riquet. The removal of M. Bergeret's household to Paris, where he has been appointed Professor at the Sorbonne, is related entirely from Riquet's point of view. On principle, Riquet objects to removals, and his principles are fortified by experience when he finds himself put into a trunk by his mistress, Pauline. Riquet's philosophy is admirably expounded in this volume. He "had a religious nature which rendered divine honours to man. He considered his master to be great and kind, but it was when he saw him at table that Monsieur Bergeret's greatness and kindness appealed to him most. If human things appeared to him inestimably precious, the articles of human food seemed to him august." Riquet's mind worked in the same direction as Caliban's, whose "brave god" was the sailor Stephano, the bearer of "celestial liquor." Caliban knelt to Stephano. Riquet, says Anatole France, entered Monsieur Bergeret's dining-room as if it were a temple; "he approached the table as if it were an altar. During the meal, silent and motionless, he kept his place at his master's feet."

No work in French literature paints such a vivid picture of present-day provincial life in France as the volumes of *L'Histoire Contem-*

poraine. The petty intrigues and squabbles of such an existence are illustrated in the competition for the bishopric of Turcoing, for which there are two rival candidates: the Abbé Lantaigne, supported by military influence, and the Abbé Guitrel, backed by a group of rich Israelitish financiers. The contest long remains uncertain; but, in the end, it is Monsieur Guitrel who wears the coveted episcopal ring, *l'anneau d'améthyste*, which gives its title to the third volume of *L'Histoire Contemporaine.* In his description of these wealthy Jews, Monsieur France employs to the full his power of irony. In such a spirit is the character of M. le Préfet Worms-Clavelin depicted in the eighth chapter of *L'Orme du Mail.* Readers of *The Yellow Book* will remember that this chapter made its first appearance in the fifth volume of that publication in 1895. In the Jewish religion, as well as in the Jewish people, our author evinces deep interest. With their sacred writings, the Old Testament, and the rabbinical books, he is well acquainted. Their conception of God, as embodied in the Pentateuch, he boldly criticises in a manner which may justify the application to himself of the description he gives of the

Abbé Coignard: "The characteristic in which he was most utterly wanting was the sense of veneration. Nature had refused it to him, and he never made any attempt to acquire it." In *La Rôtisserie de la Reine Pédauque* ironical allusions to the Old Testament are frequent. His treatment of Christianity is hardly more reverential. Yet such a passage as the expanded story of Paul's trial by Gallio in *Sur la Pierre Blanche* proves the truth of the statement, made by a fellow novelist, that "Monsieur France is a pagan, but a pagan constantly haunted by the pre-occupation of Christ."

Monsieur France's interest in the Jews took practical form in the Dreyfus crisis, frequently discussed in the volumes of *L'Histoire Contemporaine*. *L'Affaire* was in its most acute stage when those volumes were appearing. Anatole France was one of those heroic figures who, braving that most difficult of all charges to face, the charge of a lack of patriotism, publicly espoused throughout the cause of Alfred Dreyfus.

Then for the first time in his life, Monsieur France found himself working side by side with one who had formerly been his literary enemy, Emile Zola. When, in the autumn of

1902, Zola met with his tragic death, Monsieur France delivered in the cemetery of Mont Martre an eloquent oration, never to be forgotten by those who heard it. "When the work of justice and redress," to use his own words, was at last complete, and Alfred Dreyfus was reinstated in his military rank on the 21st July 1906, Anatole France was one of the first to receive the injured man's thanks. "You yourself," said Dreyfus, "contributed powerfully to the work." "What I did, after all, was very little," was the writer's characteristically modest reply.

But we must return to Monsieur Bergeret: having taken him to Paris, and established him in the Elysium of professors, the Sorbonne, Monsieur France bade him farewell. Judging from the space he occupies, one may conjecture that Monsieur Bergeret is as great a favourite with the writer as he has become with the writer's public. *L'Histoire Contemporaine* was completed in 1901. Between 1901 and 1906 Monsieur France published but three volumes of note. The historian's rather than the novelist's task was now engrossing him: he was preparing his *Vie de Jeanne d'Arc*, a work in two volumes, which did not appear till early in 1908. In the history of the legend of Joan of Arc, and indeed in the study of history, this is an epoch-making book. For years the author had been examining the story of the Maid in ancient documents, and visiting those parts of France through which she passed. He had been bringing himself into touch with her age by gazing on pictures and other objects handed down from her time. He had resolved to forget modern science, to think the thoughts of the fifteenth century, and to efface his own personality. But, as he himself wrote years ago, *On ne sort jamais de soi-même*; and readers of *The Life of Joan of Arc* will be glad that beneath the simplicity of the mediæval narrative there may still be discerned the delicious irony and the delicate subtle humour of the novels.

The three volumes of fiction that have appeared since 1901 are *Histoire Comique*, a study of the artistic temperament, as it is observed in a talented Parisian actress; a collection of tales entitled *Crainquebille*, *Putois*, *Riquet et Plusieurs autres Récits profitables*; and *Sur la Pierre Blanche*, a series of reflections connected only by the slightest apology for a plot. Of the comparative merit of these three volumes there can be no question; the second is vastly superior to the other two. The tales vary greatly in excellence: *Crainquebille*, *Putois*, and the *Reflections of Riquet* are the best. Crainquebille, the costermonger, crushed by the unjust application of the law, is the Dreyfus case in the gutter. Putois, the inimitable story of the gardener who never existed, combines the Gallic wit of the old fabliaux with the more delicate humour of our own day. In Riquet's Reflections we are introduced to our old friend once more suffering the horrors of household removal, enduring them with canine philosophy, and sagely meditating on the problems of canine existence. On the other hand, *Histoire Comique* is hardly worthy of the author's genius, is, in fact, the only one of his works we could have done without, notwithstanding its vivid pictures of green-room life, echoes of the writer's own experience in the rehearsing and acting of his plays.[1] *Sur la Pierre Blanche*, although it contains passages of deep interest and perfect form, is not, on the whole, equal to its prototype, *Le Jardin d'Épicure*. One of

[1] Anatole France's acted plays are *Le Lys Rouge*, *Les Noces Corinthiennes*, and *L'Affaire Crainquebille*. As a dramatist, he has never been brilliantly successful.

the most exquisitely harmonious passages in the later novel is that describing the early morning at Corinth at the time of Paul's trial before Gallio.

"Gradually the town awoke. The harsh neighing of a horse rent the morning air, and there began to be heard the dull roll of wheels, the voices of drivers, and the cries of herb-sellers. Coming forth from their hovels among the ruins of the Sisyphus palace, blind old women bearing copper vessels on their heads and led by children, were going to draw water from the fountain of Pirene. On the flat roofs of the houses bordering the proconsul's garden, Corinthian women were stretching out linen to dry, and one of them was beating her child with the stems of leeks. In the deep-cut road leading to the Acropolis, an old man, half naked, bronzed by the sun, was goading the back of an ass loaded with lettuces, and was singing a slave's song through his jagged teeth into his rough beard :—

> 'Labour, little ass, as I have laboured,
> And it will profit you, you may be sure.'"

Such a picture, which recalls many a passage in Renan, reveals all the elements of France's genius: his rhythmic prose, his descriptive power, and his erudition, never pedantic by reason of his intense humanity.

Monsieur France's public discourses are almost as interesting as his written works. One of his publishers, Monsieur Pelletan, has rendered a most valuable service by collecting these speeches, and publishing them in a series of volumes, illustrated by excellent portraits.

Monsieur France is a socialist. "Wealth and poverty," he teaches, "are crimes, and charity greatly increases the crime. The rich give a little in order that they may keep much." Whether or not we agree with this doctrine, its enunciation by such a profound thinker as Monsieur France makes it at least worth consideration, especially in these days when we too often endeavour to hide our social abuses by gigantic schemes of charity, which, it is quite obvious, only increase the evil. When Monsieur Bergeret gave two sous to a beggar he felt he had committed a crime.

A thinker so far in advance of his day, an author so vastly superior to the multitude of writers, a philosopher seeing deep into the heart of things, Monsieur France directs our glance to the future. Towards what sort of a world are we moving? What will be the result of tendencies which, deny them as we may, oppose them as we do, are nevertheless developing fast year by year? What will they bring to us? These are questions which the reading of Monsieur France's novels almost inevitably suggest.

In the last chapter of his last volume, *Sur la Pierre Blanche*, in a vision entitled, "Through the Gate of Ivory or of Horn," Anatole France sketches the world of the future: a world of flying machines, of social equality, of life in common: an essentially clean and healthy world: and yet a cold world, an uninteresting and unromantic world it seems to us. We cling naturally to our present evils; we hug closely the injustices and the humbugs of our present social system. Of course we should feel out of it in the Europe of 2270. "The rule of the proletariat is certain to come," writes our author. He thinks it will establish justice. Will it? The nobility have had their day at governing the world, the middle class theirs. It is just that the people's turn should come. Will they do better than their predecessors? Monsieur France thinks they will. This confident faith in future justice differs widely from the despondent and cynical spirit of his earlier writings, of *Le Jardin d'Épicure*, for example, where he derives no hope from the continuation of the eternal flux of things, and where he defines organic life as "an accident which has happened to this ball of mud of which we form a part." The Europe of 2270, as depicted in *Sur la Pierre Blanche*, is by no means a Utopia. Society still has many defects, but enormous progress has been made. It is natural to inquire whence comes our author's change of attitude towards the problems of life. Partly, no doubt, it results from his progress from the natural pessimism of meditative youth to the equanimity of middle age. Having been brought into closer contact with actuality, he has perceived that human life does not always work out so badly as theorists might expect; he is no longer under the dominion of abstract logic. The Dreyfus affair converted him from the armchair philosopher into a man of action. It brought him out of the study into the marketplace. From years of hard struggle against prejudice and tyranny, he derived that inspiration imparted only by strenuous effort for the common weal. Hence proceeds the more hopeful tone of his later works. *Lentement mais toujours l'humanité réalise les rèves du sage,* is a sentence in one of his most recently published discourses.

Women will naturally be interested to notice how Monsieur France has changed his opinion concerning the emancipation of their sex. Although one must always be careful not to take Monsieur France too seriously, in *Le Jardin d'Épicure* there is a passage which can hardly be wholly sarcastic, where he maintains that women lose their charm and their power over men when they do men's work.

"If I were you," he writes, addressing women, "I should hate those emancipators who wish to make you the equals of men. They are degrading you. A fine avocation for you to be the equal of a lawyer or a chemist! Take heed; already they have deprived you of some of your mystery and your charm. But all is not yet lost: men still fight for you, commit suicide for you, ruin themselves for you, although they have ceased to give up their seats to you in omnibuses." Judging from his attitude towards other problems, one would hardly expect Monsieur France to write in this strain nowadays. At any rate, in the Europe of 2270, there is sex equality; men and women do the same work, and women have lost none of their attractiveness thereby. One of the most delightful figures in this new world is a woman electrical engineer.

It is impossible to classify Anatole France as a writer. He stands absolutely alone. He belongs to no school. He is no realist like so many of his contemporaries; neither is he an impressionist like Pierre Loti, nor a moralist like Paul Bourget. If we must put him in some pigeon-hole in present-day French fiction, we shall not go far wrong in regarding him as the pioneer of that classical reaction which is now dawning in French literature. He is the very embodiment of the artistic temperament, and a classicist not only in the fine polish and finish of his phrase, but in the spirit of his writings.

One of his greatest attractions lies in the delicate irony, no less subtle than that of Rabelais and Voltaire, which permeates all his work. Indeed, with these two great masters of French prose Monsieur France has much in common. His style is equally forcible. His humour is as essentially Gallic, and therefore as likely to offend Anglo-Saxon notions of decorum. His zeal in attacking all abuses, no matter how firmly they be rooted in the pride and prejudice of the day, is equally fearless.

Geniuses, we are told, do not understand themselves. They must not therefore expect others to understand them. For an ordinary mortal to attempt to explain a genius is like endeavouring to describe all the glittering surfaces of a crystal as it flashes its myriad facets in the sunlight. For this reason, if for no other, these considerations of Monsieur France's writings must necessarily be very imperfect. They may be appropriately closed by quoting his own estimate of his work, all too modest, but accurate as far as it goes: "You will find in my writings," he says, "perfect sincerity (lying demands a talent I do not possess), much indulgence, and some natural affection for the beautiful and good."

Whilst this volume has been passing through the press, arrangements have been made for the publication by Mr. Lane of an English translation of the works of M. Anatole France.

MARCEL PRÉVOST

THE WORKS OF MARCEL PRÉVOST

1887. **Le Scorpion.**
1888. **Chonchette.**
1889. **Mademoiselle Jaufre.**
1890. **Cousine Laura.**
1891. **La Confession d'un Amant.**
1892. **Lettres de Femmes.**
1893. **L'Automne d'une Femme.**
1894. **Les Demi-Vierges.**
Nouvelles Lettres de Femmes.
1895. **Notre Compagne.**
1897. **Dernières Lettres de Femmes.**
Le Jardin Secret.
1898. **Trois Nouvelles.**
1900. **Les Vierges Fortes** { **Frédérique.** **Léa.** }
L'Heureux Ménage.
1901. **Le Domino Jaune, les Palombes.**
1902. **Le Pas Relevé.**
Lettres à Françoise.
1904. **La Princesse d'Erminge.**
1905. **L'Accordeur Aveugle.**
1906. **Monsieur et Madame Moloch.**
1907. **Femmes.**
1908. **Lettres à Françoise Mariée.**

MARCEL PRÉVOST, 1862

"The Passions must be purified. They may all become innocent if well directed and controlled."—JOUBERT.

MARCEL PRÉVOST is the most essentially French of contemporary French writers. Only English readers thoroughly conversant with the inevitable trend of the Latin temperament will escape being shocked by many of his novels. Prévost is not merely French, he is French eighteenth century. Like many a novelist of that period, he owes much to that so-called model of propriety, our own Samuel Richardson. With the exceptions of *Les Demi Vierges* and *Lettres de Femmes*, readers of certain pages of *Pamela* will discover nothing more indecorous in any of the novels of Prévost; and they will find the French novelist's moral tone infinitely higher than Richardson's, for Prévost never sinks to the utilitarianism of *Pamela*, advocating honesty because it is the best policy.

Prévost, on the contrary, has a high ethical

ideal. He proudly calls himself the disciple of George Sand and Dumas *fils*. His novels are written with the purpose of conveying distinct moral teaching, as he tells us in his Preface to *La Confession d'un Amant*.

"All the books," he writes, "that have profoundly moved the heart of humanity, have said to it in some way or other: here is a path you may follow. Thus to point out the road to those who walk by one's side is not to claim to have discovered it. It is merely to say like a humble pilgrim: 'I myself have travelled through this country; I know the roads and where they lead. Before you begin your journey let me tell you of mine.'"

Too often, however, one must admit, certain pitfalls on the road, which the traveller is intended to avoid, are described with unnecessary detail.

"Prévost," writes Jules Lemaître, "is a moralist who, certain of his conclusions, loves to dwell at length on what he condemns."

Following in the footsteps of *La Divine Sand* and Dumas *fils*, Prévost claims to have revived the Romantic novel, fallen into disrepute since the days of *Mauprat* and *La Dame aux Camélias*. In his Preface to

Chonchette, published in 1888, he complains that the majority of the young novelists of his generation "attempt to describe in detail the lives of people to whom nothing happens; the rest devote themselves to minute psychological analysis. . . . As for the novel properly so-called, the romantic novel, it has fallen to the inferior craftsmen of the literary art, by whom it has been discredited."

"The romantic novel," says Prévost, "is one in which imagination and observation are reconciled, in which the interest lies in the plot as well as in the description of character. It need not necessarily treat of love; in *Père Goriot*, for example, the theme is paternal affection; but it must relate a story out of the common, out of the daily routine of human passion."

Prévost is essentially a woman's novelist. His works, when they are not studies in femininity like *Les Demi Vierges* and *Les Vierges Fortes*, describe that masculine temperament which is most powerfully influenced by women, Jules Amadou in *Le Scorpion* and Count Jean de Guercelles in *Un Voluptueux*. "Love," says Prévost, "is the novel's subject *par excellence*." *Daphnis and Chloe* and

Manon Lescaut, he maintains, are types of the story which endure. He is indeed, as a recent critic has said, "an expert in the affairs of the heart, which he distils with a superior dexterity, a voluptuous sweetness, and an insinuating tenderness."

His works are a rare gallery of portraits of modern femininity, ranging from the merely sensuous Jeanne in *Le Scorpion* to the strenuous idealist Romaine Pirnitz, in the two works entitled *Les Vierges Fortes*. Not content with describing the women of to-day, Prévost in those volumes speculates concerning the women of to-morrow, and in *Les Lettres à Françoise*, like a modern Fénélon, he outlines the system of her education.

By birth and training Prévost belongs to the French civil service. His father was employed in the French excise department, and was stationed at Paris, where, on the 1st of May 1862, his son Marcel was born. A few years later Prévost *père* was transferred to Tonneins, a village in Lot et Garonne. Thus the future novelist spent the early years of his boyhood in that Gascony which figures so frequently in his books, with its white roads, its whiter dusty houses, and "its river so white that it appeared like a strip of white muslin stretched between two banks." Here the child, observant from his earliest years, had excellent opportunities for the study of that Gascon temperament which later he was to depict in his novels. "Every Gascon," he writes in *Mademoiselle Jaufre*, "presents two distinct personalities, those of *a troubadour and a commercial traveller*." The gay, swaggering *franc-gascon*, le Vidame Henri de Rocpiquet of that novel, is probably a memory of his boyhood.

Prévost received his early education at the Jesuit school, Saint Joseph de Tivoli, at Bordeaux. Unlike many literary men trained by the Society, he has remained a Catholic, at any rate in name; but he is broad-minded enough to have criticised certain institutions of the Church, and to have scandalised certain clerical circles by his first novel, *Le Scorpion*. His Christianity is of that Latin type which Anglo-Saxons find it hard to understand. To regard *le bon Dieu* as a comrade rather than a distant divinity appears to them irreverent. No orthodox English Christian, for example, would ever dream of making his heroine address the Deity in the tone of familiarity adopted by one of Prévost's characters, who prays: "My God, there has been a coldness between us during the last few years."[1] Yet to a French Catholic such a form of intercession would seem perfectly consistent with true piety.

Throughout his novels the Jesuit influences of Prévost's youth may be traced in his constant preoccupation with moral problems, in his indulgent attitude towards life, and in his belief in the relativity of ethical truth. "Truth is not, as they tell you, dazzling and precise," says George Ortsen to Léa, in *Frédérique*.

An interesting description of the boy Marcel on his arrival at his Bordeaux school has been given by one who was his schoolfellow, and is now his fellow-novelist, M. Camille Vergniol, who writes :—

"A countenance at once furious and amazed, a suit of peach-colour, of a shade so delicate, so pale! . . . the trousers of which stopped at the ankles, a little fellow with eyes blinking through shortness of sight. . . . The peach-coloured suit, and the ferocious orbs rolling behind spectacles, amused us for the rest of the week."[2]

[1] "Mon Dieu, nous sommes un peu en froid depuis nombre d'années."

[2] "Une tête à la fois furieuse et ahurie, un vêtement fleur de pècher d'un tendre ! d'un clair ! . . . dont le pantalon s'arrêtait aux chevilles, un petit bonhomme aux yeux clignotant de myope. . . . Le complet fleur de pècher, les pantalons courts et les roulements d'yeux féroces derrière les verres de lorgnon nous divertirent durant le reste de la semaine."

But the new boy's schoolmates were not long in discovering in him something more than a mere butt for their merriment. They ceased laughing when, on the Monday after his arrival, he came out top in Latin prose, and on the Monday following in Greek composition. And so it went on from Monday to Monday, until, having passed his *baccalauréat* with distinction, the time came for him to leave Bordeaux for Paris. There he entered the famous Jesuit College, l'Ecole Sainte Geneviève, which, under the alias *Ecole de la Rue des Postes*, figures in *Le Scorpion*. In that "great house of priests, with its high stone walls, surmounted by lattice-work, as if to defy any attempt to climb over," Prévost pursued his studies for the Ecole Polytechnique; and, at the age of twenty, attained the honour of passing ninety-seventh in the examination for that famous school.

His residence at the Ecole Polytechnique furnished him with that experience of French collegiate life which he was to reproduce in the pages of *Cousine Laura*.

Already in his spare moments he had begun to dabble in literature. Several of these early attempts, the first of which was entitled *Conscrard Chambergeot*, appeared while he was still at college, in *Le Clairon.* But it was not until he had left the Ecole Polytechnique, and was settled as *ingénieur des tabacs* in his childhood's home, at Tonneins, that he produced his first novel of mark, *Le Scorpion*, which first appeared in *Le Matin*, in 1886. A powerful study of character, at once psychological and physiological, *Le Scorpion* had a brilliant success, although, as we have seen, it met with hostile criticism in certain clerical circles.

Scorpion is the nickname given by students of l'Ecole des Postes to clerics in minor orders pursuing the studies of those preparing for Saint Cyr. The *Scorpion* in this case is Jules Amadou, a native of the Gascon hamlet, Nicole, not far from Tonneins.

He is one in whom the flesh and the spirit are for ever at war. From his peasant mother he inherits a devout but weak nature, from his anonymous father he receives a heritage of passion, touched with brutality. Already in the dawn of manhood the temptress is at hand in the person of the seductive Jeanne of La Maison Verte, the heiress of generations of crime, who, from the beginning, dogs the young priest's footsteps, and finally compasses his ruin.

Pity is the dominant sentiment aroused by the character of Jules. In atonement for the crime of his birth, his elder half-brother Pierre, stern and severe albeit kind-hearted, had from his cradle consecrated Jules to the priesthood. He never pauses to ask whether the boy is fitted for such a calling, and Jules never questions the wisdom of his brother's decision. His attitude is one of dumb resignation to his brother's will, until he makes the acquaintance of Pierre's friend, the Jesuit Father, Raymond Jayme. Jules is attracted by the magnetic personality of Père Jayme, under whose influence, and in opposition to his brother's wish, he decides to join the Society of Jesus. In order to escape from the evil neighbourhood of Jeanne, Jules follows Père Jayme's advice, and journeys to Paris to enter the College in La Rue des Postes. And in the first chapters we are shown the young seminarist, just arrived from his native village, simple child that he is and ignorant of life, although a youth of twenty, in his cassock grey with the dust of travel, bearing his old-fashioned valise, wandering, lost in the streets of Paris. Here and throughout the novel, Jules is a pitiable, lovable figure. He trembles at the recollection of what he had heard of the great city, down there in Gascony, how they called it "*la grande Babylone, la Sodome moderne. Derrière les façades lépreuses, son imagination devinait on ne sait quelles scènes monstrueuses—des choses comme on en voit dans les livres des confesseurs—des crimes de Gomorrhe.*"

Wandering up and down the labyrinthine streets of the left bank, his innocent ears assailed by the solicitations of street-walkers, and licentious street songs, the young novice murmurs, as if it were a charm against evil: "*Mon Dieu! ayez pitié de moi. Je suis un misérable et un lâche.*" And often in future years, when the billows of temptation roll over his soul, that same pitiful cry escapes from his lips, as he almost instinctively contrasts his high and holy calling with the frailty of his poor human nature. In the temptations that are for ever assailing this young priest, there is little to strengthen and much to discourage his fearful soul at l'Ecole des Postes. Père Jayme is ever ready to hold out a helping hand, but he is not at Paris, and when the great crisis comes he is powerless to rescue Jules until it is too late.

The character of Père Jayme is a fine creation, a rare blending of noble courage with the tenderness of a woman. He has a stern virtue, which enables him to thank God for having placed him above temptation. The other ecclesiastics in this clerical novel are well drawn: they are the brethren of l'Ecole des Postes, and the President, Père de l'Etang, tall, dignified, and handsome, a man of wide culture, charming manner, deep insight, and worldly prudence. In strong contrast to the President are the rollicking prefect with his Gascon accent, and the gentle, silent, white-haired Brother Agapit, mystic and seer. Such portraits are all the more striking because painted by one who had recently passed his youth in Jesuit school and college. During those days Prévost's mind had received impressions of the life around him which he felt bound to record in his first long novel.

Outside the Jesuit order, the country priest Pierre, Jules' elder brother, cold, unrelenting, yet affectionate, representing goodness without charm, is a well-drawn figure. With this clerical circle the lay society of the book, of course, contrasts unfavourably, for all the characters are priests or prostitutes, with the exception of one who is an escaped convict.

The novel is in many ways quite different from any other production of its author. Jeanne's character is the only link with his later work. She is the extreme personification of a type, which with modifications will occur in subsequent novels, in *Mademoiselle Jaufre*, *La Confession d'un Amant*, and *L'Automne d'une Femme*. She is the temptress, the Delilah, whom Samson in Milton's poem describes as—

> "That spacious monster, my accomplish't snare
> . . . .
> That wisest and best men full oft beguil'd."

Prévost's style remains to-day very much what it was in his first novel twenty-one years ago. Easy, fluent, picturesque, with an echo of Georges Sand, it yet occasionally lapses into affectations of modernism. Such lapses have, of course, caught the vigilant eye of that purist Jules Lemaître. "They are only too common," he bewails, "among present day authors of real talent. The writers of the past sometimes wrote weakly, they never wrote badly."

Chonchette, Prévost's second novel, appeared in 1888, the year after *Le Scorpion*, to which it is greatly inferior. Like a true romantic novel, the plot of *Chonchette* is characterised by a complete lack of verisimilitude; and it is not surprising that the author should have deemed it necessary to introduce this work by an apology for that form of literature which it is intended to revive.

In 1889 came a second work of mark, *Mademoiselle Jaufre*, one of the author's most characteristic books, and one of the most widely read of his productions. *Mademoiselle Jaufre* is a novel which has won great praise from the critics. "Monsieur Prévost has never written anything more charming than the idyll at the beginning, and nothing so profound as the ethical study which forms the most significant part of the book," writes Monsieur Pélissier. But, be it noted, this criticism was written before the appearance of *Les Vierges Fortes*, two ethical studies in fiction quite as profound and significant as *Mademoiselle Jaufre*. In this novel, the author appears definitely as a moralist. In *Le Scorpion* his criticism of life had been purely negative; his object had been to condemn the indiscriminate application of a system which he considers good in itself. In *Mademoiselle Jaufre* he has a constructive theory to propound: a theory of ethical compromise, of what he calls concession to life. *Mademoiselle Jaufre* is also his first distinctly femininist novel.

Camille Jaufre is a motherless girl, the only child of a country doctor in a Gascon village. Dr. Jaufre, intelligent and well-read, is imbued with the notions of Schopenhauer concerning the inferiority of woman's nature and the imperfectibility of her will. His daughter's future functions he believes to be solely those of wife and mother. For women his ethical code is beyond doubt short and simple; it comprises merely a horror of untruth, desire for marriage, and love of home. While religious and intellectual culture find no place in his daughter's education, while her mind is allowed to form itself haphazard, the greatest care and attention are devoted to her physical development.

According to the author, this system of education is entirely responsible for all that follows. Camille falls a victim to the first unscrupulous man she meets, who abandons her when he discovers she is about to suffer the consequences of her action. Her betrayer has appealed to her senses alone. Her heart is won by the playmate of her childhood, Louis

Lhote, who has idealised her as the very personification of perfect purity and goodness. Camille welcomes marriage with Louis, not only as the realisation of her love, but as a means of hiding her fault. Concealing her condition from her lover, she allows herself to marry him. And he, when he discovers her deception, in an agony of despair and disillusionment, leaves his wife, as he believes, for ever.

"I entreat you," writes Jules Lemaître in his criticism of this novel,[1] "not to judge this beautiful unfortunate creature too harshly. She does hateful things without becoming hateful."

"Camille's story," he continues, "is that of an irreflective creature, very close to nature, by no means bad at heart, transformed by her very fall, and by the horrible lie to which this fall constrains her, into a being capable of loving and leading a moral life."

Camille has indeed to learn by her own bitter experience what her father had failed to teach her.

The moral evolution of Camille's husband, Louis Lhote, is as interesting as that of

[1] *Les Contemporains*, fifth series.

Camille herself. The dawn of love in Louis' heart is described with the author's subtle insight, as also are his sentiments towards Camille after he has discovered her treachery: his love persists; he finds infidelity to her impossible, and gradually he feels an uncontrollable desire to return and forgive. He confides in his friend, Robert Claeys; and in the advice Robert gives we recognise that indulgent attitude towards life which, derived by the author from his Jesuit instructors, is the fundamental teaching of this book. "From the point of view of rigorous morals," says Claeys, "such a return is a concession and a weakness; but these concessions to life are indispensable. . . . The important point is to know why one makes them, and to make them consciously, not by a reflex action of the will."

Prévost's earliest works had been written as more or less of a pastime, in the leisure left after the accomplishment of his official duties. About 1890 he left the civil service and became a professional man of letters. In this year and the following he published two novels of no great importance, *Cousine Laura* and *La Confession d'un Amant.* The last has been described as morally the most suspicious of all his works. But that accusation may be brought with equal justice against *Les Demi Vierges*, a novel which appeared three years later and contributed greatly to his fame. While from a literary point of view this work is brilliant, full of vivacity and keen insight, from an ethical standpoint it is hard to justify. When the author attempts to do so in his preface, he fails conspicuously. It is all very well for him to explain the high moral purpose with which the novel was written, the work remains likely to do more harm than good. *Les Demi Vierges* is a striking illustration of Lemaître's criticism that Prévost loves to dwell on what he condemns.

The subject of the novel is the degeneration of the young girl of fashionable society. Hector le Tessier, a cynical man of the world, describing Parisian society to a young aristocrat recently arrived from the provinces, announces the bankruptcy of two institutions: "first," he says, "there is *le krack de la pudeur;* secondly, *le krack de la dot.* No one now hesitates to repeat yesterday's social scandals before the young girl of the period. There are no plays to which she is not taken. There are no novels that she has not read." The dowry of £240 a year that used to be considered sufficient for a millionaire's daughter is now barely enough to pay for the hire of her carriage. The young girl, no longer educated in a convent, according to what Hector le Tessier thinks "the excellent system" of former times, grows up in the wealth and luxury it has taken her parents forty years to acquire; and she refuses to marry until she can find a husband capable of securing for her the same luxurious ease in the married state. The young girl of the past generation, "a little white goose," fresh from her convent school, ignorant of life, and married out of hand, was by no means ideal, but she was infinitely superior to her successor, the hardened flirt of to-day.

"The fault," says Prévost in his preface, "lies with the mothers, and the remedy is in their hands: they must live with their daughters the lives of young girls. If they lack the courage to make this sacrifice, then, 'for mercy's sake,' he cries, 'don't introduce them into your society life, don't accustom them to live like married women. Marry them young, and keep them out of society till they are married. As a means of education nothing is so good as serious family life; nevertheless, a well-managed school is always better than an idle home, open to all books and to all kinds of people. 'But we must teach them life!' No, madame, you must teach them duty, honour, resignation."

Now we see Prévost on the full tide of femininism. *Le Jardin Secret*, a fine novel published in 1898, treats of the equality of the sexes before the moral law. So far there had seemed to Prévost only one destiny for women; that of marriage. "Marry your daughters and marry them young" is, as we have seen, his constant admonition to mothers. But the dawn of a new century seems to have brought to him the dawn of a new idea: about 1900 he begins to realise that all women cannot marry, because there are not enough men to go round. This reflection inspires him to write his most serious novel, *Les Vierges Fortes*, two volumes entitled, the first *Frédérique*, the second *Léa*, which appeared in 1900. They deal with the great problems of femininism: the economic independence of woman, the equality of the sexes, the purification of the marriage ideal. True Latin as he is, Prévost barely touches on the question which for the moment is agitating the Anglo-Saxon femininists, woman's right to citizenship. Neither does he attempt a solution of the problem of woman's economic independence. All that he does is to prove that we are passing through a transition stage of experiments and failures, but that he believes in the ultimate evolution of a type of womanhood higher than any the world has yet seen.

"Every femininist reformation must begin in the school, where the woman-child learns a trade and a doctrine," writes Prévost in *Léa*. And the history of such a school is the main theme of these volumes. In *Léa* Prévost relates how two Austrian women, Romaine Pirnitz and Herminie Sanz, imbued with the principles of John Stuart Mill's *Subjection of Women*, and having studied femininist movements in England, America, and Scandinavia, found a college at Buda Pesth. Then, when their efforts are crowned with success, they confide the direction of the work to others, while they go to London. There they found "Free College," of which Herminie Sanz becomes the directress. Pirnitz meanwhile establishes herself at Paris. She studies the various femininist groups of the French capital, not with the object of joining any one of them, but rather that she may select suitable helpers from among their members. In the tumult of congresses and meetings, however, she finds few. It is from the quieter walks of life that she recruits her lieutenants. In the following pages Prévost describes the women whom Pirnitz selects to be her fellow-workers in the femininist cause. And here he presents us with a portrait gallery of striking feminine types drawn to the life, which is one of his greatest literary achievements.

"Pirnitz's choice fell first on a former government teacher, Mademoiselle Heurteau, very intelligent, imbued with emancipated ideas, and on her friend, Duyvecke Hespel, the daughter of agriculturists in the neighbourhood of Hazebroucke, who had come to the capital to be trained as a teacher. Elsewhere Pirnitz met at Paris the eldest sister of a certain Edith Craggs, whom she had known in London in Methodist circles. Daisy Craggs was an Irishwoman of about forty; during her youth she had taken part in the nationalist agitation of her country; now, schooled by life's lessons, she was only revolutionary in conversation; she was earning her living by translating and contributing to foreign newspapers. A passionate philanthropist, she had adopted a ward of the Society for the Protection of Children, Geneviève Soubize, the daughter of confirmed drunkards, herself extremely neurotic. Daisy's devoted affection had transformed the peevish, petulant little hussy into a vivacious, intelligent young woman. Daisy's maternal care had cured Geneviève of her hysteria. Geneviève adored her benefactress, for whom she would have suffered death without a moment's hesitation. Geneviève had now completed her studies at the Faculty and gained her midwife's diploma.

"Mlle. Heurteau, Duyvecke Hespel, Geneviéve, and Daisy were Pirnitz's first recruits. . . . Meanwhile the apostle was seeking the funds necessary for the foundation of a school: a newspaper advertisement placed her in communication with Mlle. de Sainte-Parade, who was delighted with Pirnitz and her projects. All this was much, but it was not enough. Pirnitz had no longer Herminie Sanz at her side; and neither Daisy, nor Geneviève, nor Duyvecke, nor even Mlle. Heurteau represented those ardent helpers for whom she longed. She would not begin the work until she had found them."

The circumstances of her chance meeting with the two beautiful sisters, Frédérique and Léa, are related in the novel which bears Frédérique's name. To return to the passage we are quoting from *Léa* :—

"Pirnitz recognised in the two sisters just those helpers for whom she was seeking. A series of imperious fatalities had fashioned the elder's noble soul, had revealed to her, when she was still a child, her own conscience; and her woman's personality, had caused her to revolt against the slavery of women imposed by man: in her turn Frédérique had moulded according to her own image the sweeter, more impressionable, soul of her younger sister. . . . The sisters, who bore the same name, knew they were not the daughters of the same father. They were aware of the vulgar calamity that had dishonoured their home. . . . As for Léa, she, like Frédérique, had determined never to marry: the two sisters always together would live one for the other. . . . Pirnitz all unconsciously revealed to them the very ideal for which they were seeking: that of a life devoted not merely to the defence of themselves against men, but to the protection of their innumerable sisters weaker than they.

"Initiated by the apostle into her projects, introduced to Mlle. de Sainte-Parade, they took part in the inception of the school; it was even Frédérique who proposed the site . . . and conducted the negotiations for its acquirement."

"Women taught by women in complete independence" is the principle of the institution which goes by the name of School of the Arts of Women.

On the opening day Pirnitz, the orator of the group, who, although plain—almost deformed—was possessed of a wonderful magnetic personality, defined the ideal of *La Vierge Forte*:—

"As long as woman's cause remains unwon," says Pirnitz, "it is necessary that certain women should take up that cause, should constitute themselves its advocates and its priestesses. And who can adapt herself better to such a double rôle than the woman voluntarily excluded from marriage and from family life, or at least accepting serenely, without regrets, an exclusion imposed upon her by circumstances."

"To such a woman all women will be sisters, and all young girls will be one immense family to whom she will consecrate herself with disinterested devotion. She will be the ideal at once of the strong woman and the holy virgin of the Scriptures. This celibate, proud of her celibacy, will travel through life assailed by none of its dangers : she will point out the way of liberty and serenity.

. . . . . .

"The crowd will regard her always as a grand exception, and there is no danger of such an exception becoming the rule. But I persist in believing that gradually such women will come to form a kind of feminine aristocracy, an indispensable bond of union, so to speak, between the various social groups, the inspirer, the consoler of humanity."

Pirnitz is the only member of the group who completely realises this high ideal. The School of the Arts of Women ends in failure. For finally the femininists are forced to abandon the work, which is taken over by the government educational authorities. The founders of the school make enemies by flaunting their independence of masculine support in the face of state and municipal officials. Yet they are not really independent: their neighbour, the rich manufacturer, Duramberty, the former employer of Frédérique and her sister, is in love with Frédérique. He is their ground landlord, who has permitted them to rent the site of their school on very easy terms; but, when Frédérique rejects his attentions, his proposal of an irregular union and even his offer of marriage, he ceases to associate himself with the work. By withdrawing his support he unchains against it the hounds, hitherto held in leash, of political jealousy, ecclesiastical prejudice, and financial embarrassment.

Before the actual ruin of the institution takes place, it has already been abandoned by three of the femininist group. Duyvecke has obeyed her maternal instinct, and married an artisan in order that she may tend his motherless boy; the neurotic Geneviève Soubize, agitated by the impending ruin of the school, and missing the quiet home life that her protector had given her before its foundation, loses her mental balance, and narrowly escapes death beneath the guillotine; Daisy Craggs withdraws from the work to devote her life to her demented protégée; Mademoiselle Heurteau intrigues with the educational authorities on her own account, and when the crisis comes, is employed by them to carry on the school as a government institution.

Even of the three remaining who are apparently true to the cause, one is at heart a traitor. Léa murmurs: "I also long for freedom. I am determined to have the liberty I need and which is my due."

The book in truth shows that since the foundation of the school, Léa's life has been one long struggle to live up to the ideal of *La Vierge Forte*. She has been endeavouring vainly to drive from her heart her love for Georg Ortsen, a Finlander, whom she had met when she and Frédérique had been living in London. Thus upon the altar of femininism she had sacrificed herself and her lover, who had wished to make her his wife. But Léa's sacrifice had been a dismal failure. Her heart had never been in the work. And now she throws away the mask, and, leaving her sister and Pirnitz, seeks Georg in London.

After many months she finds him, but not until it is too late, and consumption has made terrible ravages on her feeble frame.

Léa's short married life, blissful and dignified, though passed in the shadow of the tomb, illustrates the author's ideal of woman's emancipation in marriage. If Pirnitz stands for the future Eve, Georg is the future Adam. In him man ceases to be woman's adversary. "I know that you are my equal," he says to Léa. "There is no need for you to revolt in order to prove it. Henceforth your love for me will involve no slavery."

The intense and prolonged pathos of these closing chapters of the last volume of *Les Vierges Fortes* is a serious fault in the book. As Stevenson says, "we can no longer endure to wallow naked in the pathetic." No wonder that, after writing these pages, the author suffered a nervous breakdown, and was advised by his doctor to flee from Paris and divert his mind by writing something, no matter what, as long as it was entirely different from *Les Vierges Fortes*.

Léa's pitiful death and the tragedy of Geneviève Soubize are the Nemesis attending the attempt to force the ideal of *La Vierge Forte* upon those who are unfitted for it. Frédérique, when it is too late, realises the disastrous influence she has exercised over her sister. "It is I who have killed Léa," she cries; "but for me she would long ago have been Georg's wife, and nothing of what has overwhelmed her would have happened." Madame Sanz had already seen that *La Vierge Forte* "cannot be forced like a hot-house plant, but must bloom spontaneously."

Among the striking types of femininity described in these volumes there are two that have an air of unreality. From the days of John Wesley, Methodism has always been an exotic in France. In the character of Edith Craggs the author has failed to catch the note of English Methodism. The preaching tone is slightly overdone. It is a caricature not a portrait of an unctuous Methodist that represents her saying to a porter, when she gives him twopence—

"We, like the apostle, have neither gold nor silver. But what we have we give you. If you are not too tired, one evening this week, come to our workmen's institute. . . . You will there find refreshment and distraction without sin."

In another direction the character of Tinka Ortsen, Georg's sister, also lacks probability; for a good woman like Tinka it would be impossible to abandon her own two children, because her husband refused to acknowledge his natural child by another woman. Fortunately for the sake of verisimilitude, Tinka repents later of the error of her ways; and, by returning to her husband and children, she obtains that justice for the wronged child which her unnatural conduct had failed to procure.

The chapters in these two volumes descriptive of English life, lack reality generally through incorrectness of detail. Why will our neighbours persist in imagining that we eat *pudding* at tea? Our London seasons may be backward, but our chestnut Sunday rarely occurs so late as the last week in June. These are but minor blemishes, however, and they do not prevent *Les Vierges Fortes* from remaining the author's most significant work, a powerfully depicted episode in that great human drama, the eternal warfare between the sexes.

The system of Romaine Pirnitz had failed to produce the kind of woman at which it aimed. The conclusions of *Les Vierges Fortes* are chiefly negative. In a novel, entitled *Lettres à Françoise*, published in 1902, the author grows constructive; he sketches an outline of what appears to him a scheme of healthy feminine education. Here he falls back on his nineteenth century idea, that marriage and maternity are necessarily woman's destiny; he leaves the bachelor woman out of account; perhaps he will deal with her education in another volume.

The Françoise, to whom these letters are written, is a girl of eighteen, just completing her school education, at l'Institution Berquin, Rue de Ranelagh, Paris. Her uncle, a middle-aged bachelor and man of the world, writes to his niece fortnightly letters intended to fill up the gaps in her school education. For she complains that from her schoolmistress, Madame Rochette, she learns nothing of life.

"We are taught arithmetic, geography, sewing," she writes, "but we must not ask our good Mme. Rochette to teach us life. . . . Nevertheless I should very much like to know everything that is not wanted for examinations."

And the uncle replies that her complaint is perfectly just; "a town, a society, a nation, a period are around you," he writes, "and you are separated from it by a veritable air-tight partition, which one day will be taken down, because you have had the good luck to pass some examination. I agree it is absurd." And so, in order to complete his niece's education, he writes at length of education, dress, balls, sport, and marriage.

He encourages Françoise to be modern. "Keep your taste for novelty, your trust in to-morrow, your instinctive faith in the world's progress. . . . Experiment courageously in the fashions of the day, be curious about the time in which you live; you will have time enough to become reactionary." He fears that Françoise is too fond of dress. She must be *coquette*, but only in a certain manner, aiming always at what is cleanly, becoming, harmonious, avoiding all extravagance and affectation. And he prophesies that the evolution of the New Woman, which is every day bringing tailor-made clothes into greater favour, will end by ousting all other feminine attire.

This uncle, with the characteristically long views of Frenchmen, is already thinking of Françoise the Second, who figures frequently in these letters. For this child of a possible future, theories of education are discussed, specialisation is condemned, co-education is advocated, the advantages and disadvantages of examinations are weighed in the balance.

When Françoise marries, the uncle, unlike the old-fashioned Frenchman, expects her to choose her own husband. She is not to be too much influenced in her choice by financial considerations. And, once having chosen, her marriage need not be hurried; for he considers that the long engagements common on the other side of the Channel have much to recommend them.

Françoise had meanwhile already met her fate in Mme. Rochette's parlour, in the person of the brother of one of her schoolfellows, a young St. Cyrien, "*qui est si bien, si bien,*" she writes to her uncle. And, so like an old-fashioned love story, the book ends with her marriage to her friend's brother.

This volume is interesting throughout. While giving the author's ideas on female education, it presents an excellent picture of the French middle-class healthy young schoolgirl of the present day.

Four years after the appearance of *Les Lettres à Françoise,* Prévost struck a distinctly new note in another novel, *Monsieur et Madame Moloch.* Here we are no longer occupied with femininism. It is not the psychology of woman but of the modern German nationality that is the theme of this book.

Prévost, like many of his contemporaries in

France, considers Germany to be passing through a phase of intellectual and artistic decline. Once, in the days of Goethe and Heine, Beethoven and Bach, Germany was the home of the Idea; now since the Prussian domination the Idea has been succeeded by Brute Force.

But *Monsieur et Madame Moloch* is not merely occupied with German psychology. It is essentially a romantic novel, which in many of its pages recalls the *Prisoner of Zenda.* Its humour is delicious. Its descriptive passages are poetical and picturesque. The character of the old professor, Monsieur Moloch, is one of the author's most delightful creations. There is also a young French school-girl, clever, *coquette*, impulsive, and most charming, who has many points in common with the Françoise of the letters. The construction of the plot proves the correctness of a judgment lately passed upon Prévost: "that he is one of those rare recent writers who are scrupulous concerning the warp and woof of their plots."

We have now considered all Prévost's serious works. As well as novels he has published several volumes of short stories, in which he reveals the talent of the French conteur, inherited from mediæval predecessors and spiced with the true Gallic wit. Something of this talent is to be observed in three volumes, *Lettres de Femmes*, which appeared in 1893, 1894, and 1897. These letters have nothing in common with *Les Lettres à Françoise*. They are characterised by a prurient puerility which denies them any claim to rank as literature. Had they been the work of an English writer critics might have whispered that they were mere *pot-boilers*. Possibly it is on account of such works as these that their author has not yet entered "the home of all the proprieties" and joined the company of the Immortals, an honour which he would otherwise have merited.

His latest production is a volume of tales entitled *Femmes*. The first story, *Un Voluptueux*, is the longest and the most striking in the book. The character of the Voluptuary, Count Jean de Guercelles, a modern dandy of over forty, is the author's contribution, so he tells us in the preface, to that psychology of the Don Juan which has occupied so many eminent writers from the sixteenth century down to our own day. And here we may remark what has been recently set forth in an interesting publication,[1] the evolution through the centuries of the character of Don Juan. He has been gradually ascending the moral scale. In the nineteenth century he is not, as he was in the seventeenth, a murderer, a robber, an incendiary; rehabilitated by Romanticism, he is the hero we have not rightly understood. In Prévost's story he is the Voluptuary on the way to reformation. "Have I not been a dupe?" he asks himself at the end, "the dupe of others and of myself, the dupe of verbal conventions, which call love that which is not love?"

His awakening he owes to a woman, Henriette Deraisme. In earlier novels Prévost has shown us the dawn of true love in the heart of an unsophisticated high-minded youth, Louis Lhote in *Mademoiselle Jaufre*, Georg Ortsen in *Les Vierges Fortes*. In *Un Voluptueux* we have the mature unprincipled man of the world. After a life of fashionable profligate idleness, he obtains his first glimpse of what love really is and what it may mean to a man. The woman from whom too late he receives this revelation is a type such as Françoise's uncle

[1] Cp. *La Légende de Don Juan, son Evolution dans la Littérature, des Origines au Romantisme*, par Georges Gendarme de Bévotte.

would have his niece to be, high-minded, intelligent, independent, acute, loving purity above all things, and for its sake ready to sacrifice her heart's desire; Henriette is one of the noblest characters in the author's procession of femininity.

As he advances in his literary career Monsieur Prévost shows less and less of that tendency to dwell on human perversity which we have already deplored. *Frédérique* and *Léa*, which by the way have been translated into English, are novels of high seriousness. *Les Lettres à Françoise* and *Monsieur et Madame Moloch* are essentially wholesome; and these four volumes at least may be safely recommended to English readers.

PIERRE DE COULEVAIN .

THE WORKS OF PIERRE DE COULEVAIN.

1898. **Noblesse Américaine.**
1901. **Eve Victorieuse.**
1904. **Sur la Branche.**
1906. **L'Ile Inconnue.**

PIERRE DE COULEVAIN

"Whatever he may do man is always and before all things the representative of his race."—GUSTAVE LE BON.

FRANCE is the land of femininity not of feminism. Femininity is Latin and Catholic; feminism is Anglo-Saxon and Protestant, writes Madame de Coulevain. England represents the masculine sex in humanity, France the feminine. There is, therefore, no need for feminism in France, where, according to Laurence Sterne, nothing but the monarchy was ever Salic.

A Frenchwoman is so absolutely a queen in her home and in society, that when she descends from her double throne to compete with men in professional life, she is inclined to be ashamed of her sex; from the days of Georges Sand downwards she has attempted to conceal it: in past generations beneath garments of masculine cut, now beneath a masculine *nom de guerre.* Thus Madame de Peyrebrune writes under the pseudonym of "Georges de Peyrebrune," Madame de Regnier under "Gérard d'Houville," and Madame Favre de Coulevain under "Pierre de Coulevain."

For at least four centuries women have adorned the literary profession in France, as writers of memoirs, letters, and above all, novels. Now there is a group of brilliant women poets. But it is still in the novel that women are producing their best work. There they find full scope for that insight into character which is their greatest literary gift. Among the most famous women writers in France to-day are Madame Edmond Adam, Madame Gyp, Madame Marcelle Tinayre, Madame Rachilde, and Madame de Noailles, who is also a poet.

In the present transition stage of the French novel there are those who think that from women will proceed the new inspiration which is hourly expected. The weakness of contemporary women novelists is the ever-resounding personal note of their writings. It seems impossible for Frenchwomen to attain to objectivity in literature.

Madame de Coulevain is a novelist whose works are read more abroad than in France. She is too cosmopolitan for her countrymen, who are an essentially self-centred nation. "Why do you want to write of Pierre de Coulevain?" more than one Parisian has asked the present writer. "No one knows her, no one reads her here." Nevertheless, the French Academy has done justice to her work, and crowned her novel, *Ève Victorieuse*, which has been translated into English by Miss Alys Hallard.

Madame de Coulevain's cosmopolitanism a stumbling-block in France, is in England and America a sign of grace. She herself realises its advantages and disadvantages. "It is at once a happiness and a misfortune," she writes. "One's faculties develop more rapidly. . . . But one inspires one's compatriots with mistrust and envy." The woman writer, Jean Noël in *Sur la Branche*, is welcomed, received, and entertained by foreigners abroad; but, when she returns to a purely French environment, she is horrified to find herself denaturalised. In conversation with persons of her own race, she wounds old sentiments and offends forgotten prejudices. The French nation is severely critical of the nomadic cosmopolitan women. "Every one should have a home, a parish, and works of charity," says a French provincial dame severely, with a significant click of her knitting-needles.

For foreigners the chief interest of Pierre de Coulevain's novels resides in their keen-sighted cosmopolitanism and strong appreciation of national character. Their plots are thin and incoherent, a mere string of loosely connected incidents, too often brought to a sudden close by some unnatural melodramatic *dénouement*. In her last volume, *L'Ile Inconnue*, the plot shrinks into an almost imperceptible thread; the characters are vague shadows. The book is indeed well described by the writer as "my visions, my impressions, and the ideas they have suggested." In truth, her novels are nothing but a series of vivid impressions. They display, as in a cinematograph, lifelike scenes of modern society, which the author intersperses with vivacious reflections on the national temperaments of the French, Italians, English, and Americans, who are the principal actors.

While certain thinkers like Mr. Andrew Lang minimise the influence of race, others, like Monsieur Gustave le Bon, assign to it great importance in the development of the species. "Every race," writes the French philosopher, "possesses a mental constitution as determined as its anatomical constitution." Madame de Coulevain agrees with her fellow-countryman. Starting from the principle of innate racial qualities, she proceeds to analyse the characteristics of Americans, French, and English. Her results are occasionally too dogmatic and far-reaching; but, on the whole, they strike one as remarkably just. In the case of Americans, she limits her observations to one particular class: the class that throngs the Rue de la Paix and the Hotel Ritz at Paris, the Carlton at London, the Palace Hotel at Aix-les-Bains. "The spending class of Americans," as Mr. H. G. Wells calls it, interests her exclusively; "the people who have largely and triumphantly got, and who with hands, pockets, safe deposit vaults full of dollars, are proceeding to realise victory."

Upon the social triumphs of these people, and especially of the women of this class, observed with considerable acuteness, Madame de Coulevain builds certain theories of humanity. For example, she considers the American millionairess, whom, from her balcony outside the Hotel Castiglione, she watches amusing herself with what Renan would call *American vulgarity*, as the necessary vehicle for the exchange of ideas between the New World and the Old.

If this theory be correct, we regret that America sends us only the froth of her social virtues, and according to the writer's own showing, keeps her more sterling excellences to herself. The woman, who is the medium of this exchange of ideas, is the elegant, travelled ultra-modern American, who, though endowed with the sound virtues of truthfulness, candour, and independence, inherited from Puritan ancestors, is nevertheless neurotic, fast, and even vulgar. She appears eager to abandon her husband and children in order to enjoy a few months' gaiety in Europe, and prepared to divorce her husband when he objects to her prolonging her absence from his fireside. The more serious type of American, strict, Puritanical, a trifle narrow, but highly cultured, generally stays at home and loves her husband and family. She does not figure in Madame de Coulevain's pages. When she does travel her favourite haunts are the libraries and museums of the Old World. She is too inartistic, too dowdily dressed, to consort with her butterfly compatriots of the Spa and casino, with whom we are chiefly concerned in these novels.

Madame de Coulevain herself has spent much of her life in these places. She lives on the wing, *Sur la Branche*, as she puts it, flitting from New York to Paris, from Paris to London, and from London to Bath, Aix, or Cannes. She has thus ample opportunities of studying the fashionable Americans, and describing their elaborate toilets, inevitable flirtations, gorgeous salons, and exquisite dressing-rooms. In such passages she rivals even that most skilful painter of modern luxury and fashion, Paul Bourget.

Madame de Coulevain is an authority on the development of certain fashionable institutions of our day. Her account in *Sur la Branche* of the evolution of *the five o'clock* in Paris is an interesting document of social history.

" Formerly Parisians used to take cake or sandwiches with a glass of Spanish wine at Gage's or Cuvillier's or at the confectioner's near the Madeleine. Now the tea-shop is an institution ; the five o'clock has become a custom. This little evolution, which has not been without its effect upon our manners, has taken place within the last fifteen years. It originated in the Rue de Rivoli, in a shop known as the Stationer's of La Concorde, kept by two

Englishmen, the brothers Neal. Were they inspired by a vision of that brown tea-pot which between half-past four and five appears in all city offices? Did they think to undertake a work of piety and profit by supplying to their compatriots the national beverage? I do not know; but there, at the end of the counter, amid books and papers, behind a screen, on two tables only, they began to serve tea and biscuits. For the first time Paris beheld a sign with the words *afternoon tea.* Tea and biscuits in a stationer's shop! Only an English brain could imagine such an invention. Never mind; the sign worked wonders. More than one Britisher on his holiday, more than one loving couple made the acquaintance of that little corner, and remember it with deep gratitude."

"This was the germ of those tea-shops which for the last three years have been growing up as quickly as mushrooms. They are to be found everywhere, in the Rue Cambon, the Rue de Rivoli, the Rue Saint Honoré, near the Louvre, and the Bon Marché. Paris has surpassed London in this respect. Does this imply that the Frenchwoman has become a tea-drinker? Not in the least; and, what is worse, she never will. She knows neither how to drink it, nor prepare it, nor pour it out. She swallows it absent-mindedly as if it were an infusion of no matter what. It excites her nerves without stimulating her. She is too fond of talking, of creating an impression, to give the necessary attention to the tea-pot, the samovar, or the kettle. She is quite incapable of repeating over and over again the liturgical questions: weak or strong? one or two lumps of sugar? cream or lemon? And when she does bring herself to ask, she never waits for an answer. The tea-shop, where, if she be not afraid of appearing too *bourgeoise*, she takes chocolate, affords her an agreeable resting-place, in the midst of her shopping and her visits to the dressmaker, and satisfies at once her desire for sociability and her exclusiveness."

The five o'clock at the Hotel Ritz is the most elegant five o'clock in Paris. There, installed in a corner, a lover of fashionable society can have an excellent view of frocks and frills and fine jewels; and from such things a keen observer, like Madame de Coulevain, is able to extract deep psychological significance. From the curl of a Frenchman's moustache she discovers his temperament. From the motion of an American rocking-chair she learns the American's state of mind. In an Englishwoman's cap, whether worn by nurse, servant, or lady of uncertain age, she sees a kind of extinguisher, extinguishing something, either independence or youth.

Madame de Coulevain, although she affects to disdain snobbery, loves the society of the rich and the high-born. "Stick to Belgravia," is her motto.

To call a person or an institution *bourgeois* is for her the very worst degree of condemnation. "Foreigners," she writes, "often ask me the meaning of the term *bourgeois*. I find it very difficult to define. . . . *Bourgeoisisme*, like provincialism, is a *mentalité*. . . . It communicates a shell-like impenetrability. Its characteristics are to be found in people who have received a superior culture, in whom are developed taste and a sense of beauty. It betrays itself by common ideas, extreme intolerance, blind obstinacy, an incapacity above all things to understand and to accord liberty. This *mentalité* creates a particular and unmistakable atmosphere. The peasant, the workman, the artisan are not *bourgeois*. I might name a king who is more so than many people born in the Rue du Sentier. Napoleon I. was *bourgeois*. Napoleon III. was not. Balzac, Guy de Maupassant were not *bourgeois;* Zola was. Two of our great newspapers, one of our best reviews are. The church of Saint Augustin is *bourgeois*, Saint Roch is not. The Comédie Française, the Opéra Comique, the Palais Royal are *bourgeois;* the Vaudeville, the Variétés, the Théatre Antoine, the cafés concerts of Montmartre are not. Among the tea-houses all are, with one exception. England, Italy, Spain, are not *bourgeoise;* Germany is and her emperor is not." Until this last sentence (thanks to Madame de Coulevain's kind explanation) we had imagined ourselves beginning to understand the meaning of this enigmatical term ; but if the German Emperor be not *bourgeois*, then we are as far from understanding the word as ever we were. Madame de Coulevain concludes by the fear that France may be becoming *bourgeoise*. "Even France! Heaven forbid."

The Americans of these novels all belong to the so-called American aristocracy. It appears to be the one nobility with which the author has no sympathy.

Of the Colonial Dames of New York, who admit to their society only such as can trace back their descent for two centuries, Madame de Coulevain writes : " Instead of creating an aristocracy of intelligence, knowledge, and talent, they have aimed at one of birth. By means of relics bought in Europe, and old family Bibles with marriages and births written on the flyleaf, they have rediscovered traces of their ancestors and laid claim to belong to existing noble families. They are prouder of being branches of an old and decayed tree than the stem of a young and vigorous plant of American growth. They are prouder of the unknown ancestor, often a useless, sometimes a bad man, than of the grandfather to whom they owe everything. And possessed by this fascinating folly, many such *parvenues* turn over church registers and the archives of the British Museum (*sic*), and, if they are clever enough, return to America with proof of their ancient origin, and sometimes with armorial bearings." When they visit Paris the ambition of these Americans, afflicted with what Pierre de Coulevain calls *aristocracy mania*, is to obtain an introduction to the Faubourg St. Germain. They regret that France is no longer an empire or a monarchy.

"Seen a live marquis," is an entry in the diary of an American beauty. And we are not surprised to find the same young lady, when later she marries an Italian nobleman, a leader of the clerical party, treacherously scheming to force her husband to accept a post offered him at court.

A court always exercises a refining elevating influence upon the neighbouring inhabitants, says an American painter in *Ève Victorieuse;* and he gives as an example the good style of the furniture to be found in the houses near Fontainebleau.

Madame de Coulevain has a great respect for what she calls *Le charme de la race.* It is obvious that her friends at Wimbledon go up several pegs in her estimation when she hears that they are descended from a noble lord whose manorial domain in the country they expect to inherit shortly. She says that she rejoices at the prospect of their good fortune simply because she does not like to see them counting shillings and pence; but we doubt whether her exultation would have been as great had the inheritance been an industrial and not a noble one.

The antipodes of Parisian life are what

most attract the wealthy American woman. She aspires to move in the high society of the Faubourg St. Germain. She also insists on observing the *demi-monde* in Parisian restaurants and music-halls.

"At home," writes Madame de Coulevain, in *Noblesse Américaine*, "she virtuously closes her door against the devil, but abroad she is enchanted to meet him. She never fails to seek him at Paris, that she may know how he looks, but especially that she may say she has seen him; and you may be sure she never finds him black enough. She buys the most daring novel, insists on seeing the most doubtful play, and generally understands neither." Hers is not the position of an English Duchess who, when offered the words of the French play she was witnessing, said: "I do not wish to understand." The American at any rate does her best to understand. She demands that the celebrities of the *demi-monde* shall be pointed out to her in the Bois. She looks at them with eager curiosity because they are so wicked. She never realises the ignominy of their lives. "Things that would for ever trouble a young French girl's soul and leave upon it ineffaceable stains pass lightly over the young American and merely amuse her. . . . She is as incapable of understanding depravity as holiness." This casual heartlessness of the rich American is illustrated in *L'Ève Victorieuse*, when three American women insist on their men taking them to a famous all-night café, Loiset's in the Rue Royale.

"'Drive to Loiset's, Rue Royale.' This order, given by Mr. Beauchamp to his coachman outside the Theatre of the Renaissance, represented another victory of woman over man. It was not without a protest that Charlie had taken his sister and Miss Carroll to the Moulin Rouge, to Olympia, and all the eccentric *cafés concerts*. He consoled himself with the thought that they, no more than he, understood the grossnesses uttered on those fashionable platforms. He was naïvely astonished at their wishing to listen in Paris to things which at New York would have made them virtuously stop their ears. Several times they had asked him to take them to the famous all-night restaurant in the Rue Royale, but he had always found an excuse for refusing.

"At Helen's request he had that evening taken a box at the Renaissance and invited the Marquis and Marchioness of Verga, with

Willie Grey. During the last *entr'acte* the three women declared that they wished to go to supper at Loiset's. They had indeed organised the plot between them, and it was necessary to yield to their persistent fancy.

"When the carriages were outside the restaurant door, two gentlemen walking up and down outside stopped to say 'good-bye.' At that moment Helen stepping on to the pavement, to her great consternation, found herself face to face with Monsieur de Limeray.

"The latter, having recognised the friends of the Marchioness of Anguilhon, hastily took leave of his companion and approached them.

"'You are not going to Loiset's?' he asked eagerly.

"'Yes, we are,' replied the Marchioness.

"'But it is not a place to be visited by respectable women.'

"'Respectable Frenchwomen,' said Madame Ronald, 'perhaps, but in us Americans respectability is so robust that we can see and hear everything. Don't you fear.'

"'But really, Helen, if this restaurant be impossible?'

"'Impossible! But all my women friends

have had supper there. It is as well known in New York as the Eiffel Tower.'

"'Well, I have never set foot in it and it is next door to my Club.'

"'Then will you come with us and eat Welsh rarebits?'

"'Here we go then for the Welsh rarebits!' said the Count. 'It is really rather amusing to see an old Parisian like me taken to Loiset's for the first time by American ladies.'

"One of the waiters took possession of the arrivals and led them to the back of the restaurant, to a kind of platform, up two steps, separated from the rest of the hall by a balustrade.

"'If you sit there,' said the waiter graciously, 'you will see everything.' These words made Monsieur de Limeray prick up his ears. He wondered what they might imply.

"Mr. Beauchamp ordered supper. The three women immediately cast a curious glance around them, and were disappointed to observe the mean proportions and the common decorations of the famous tavern.

"'Loiset's is not so beautiful,' said the Marquis Verga.

"The customers were arriving slowly;

merrymakers old and young, accompanied by women more or less pretty, more or less elegant. The hall soon grew animated by sparkling eyes, roars of laughter, outbursts of false and vulgar merriment. The atmosphere, loaded with diverse odours of smoke and strong perfumes, became close and unhealthy. . . . And all this, regarded by Monsieur de Limeray from the point of view of his sixty years, appeared hideous and heart-breaking. Charlie Beauchamp and Willie Grey were amused by the spectacle without being in the slightest perturbed by it. As for the three Americans, they picked to pieces the women's dresses, exchanged a few remarks in a low voice, chattered gaily, obviously enchanted to see so much that was shocking. In this atmosphere, overcharged with sensuality, they remained cold, dry-eyed, and serene."

L'Ève Victorieuse is Madame de Coulevain's best novel. Its chief heroine, Helen Ronald, is the most strongly drawn of her characters. Helen is slightly less frivolous and casual than the other rich American women portrayed by this author. Madame de Coulevain attributes it to the Celtic blood in her veins. Her great-grandfather was a Huguenot of Toulouse.

Worldly pleasures never entirely satisfy her. When she was a child, her brilliance at school caused it to be feared that she might become a doctor of law or of medicine, "a danger (*sic*) from which her beauty rescued her." She studied, we are told, the most extraordinary things: Buddhism, occult sciences, social questions,—studied in the manner of women, adds the author with no great loyalty to her sex. And indeed Helen's extraordinary studies do not seem to have had much effect upon her intellect. Occasionally they enable her to pose as intellectual and utter very commonplace remarks in an oracular manner intended to make them appear profound. Her masculine hearers, with gallant dissimulation, welcome these observations as if they were lights from heaven.

Helen completed her education, if it had ever been begun, in a Parisian convent. Here she attended the Protestant Church on Sunday morning, but in the afternoon went to the Catholic service, which she found "fascinating." Later in life, after her marriage, when she is troubled by an unfortunate love affair, she seeks distraction in those "fascinating" services, and goes even further: she engages a priest to instruct her in the dogmas of his faith. This ecclesiastic welcomes her as "a very Daniel" when she flippantly apologises for the Inquisition as perpetrated by Catholics who misunderstood the Church's teaching. He is, however, less pleased with his catechumen when, with unconscious irreverence, she explains away the sacraments as mere symbols. He hesitates as to whether he should admit so heretical a thinker into the bosom of the Church, but decides in the end that faith will probably come with the practice of her religion.

Helen's new religion does not, as she had hoped, restore her to wifely devotion. In the end the obsessing vision of the man who is not her husband is driven from her mind by the hypnotic touch of the Brahmin Cetteradjii.

There is no country in which psychic phenomena are studied with greater zest than in the United States, writes Madame de Coulevain. "At New York, Philadelphia, and Boston, Buddhism is in high favour. Sakya Muni has his worshippers. Bouddha, symbol of peace and repose, attracts by contrast . . . the most energetic, the most restless women of the universe." The Americans of to-day, like the Athenians of old, seek "to tell and to hear some new thing."

Helen's husband, who has all the time been unconscious of her mental disloyalty, is a famous American scientist. Deeply in love with his beautiful brilliant wife, and misled by her apparent intellectuality, he thinks her really interested in his scientific work. Every evening he sacrifices his club in order to spend the hour before dinner in his wife's dressing-room. Sitting in a rocking-chair while Helen puts the finishing touches to her toilet, he talks of politics, science, and art, while she babbles of her doings in society. "She would have been sorry to think that her husband did not permit her to share his intellectual life. Nevertheless it was only with one ear that she listened to his conversation. Fortunately, neither noticed how rare and slight was the contact of their minds."

From the talk of her scientific husband Helen picks up a few disconnected ideas, which she reproduces glibly in her conversation. Thus she makes a great impression on an elderly Parisian, an aristocratic *bon-viveur*, by describing love as a fluid which attracts one being to another. There is indeed a good deal of quasi-scientific jargon throughout these volumes. Social affinity is defined as *an isolating fluid* and so forth. Determinism in the garb of Providence is always coming in; manifestations of occultism, coincidences and prognostications are discussed in a manner that suggests the conversation of hotel *tables-d'hôtes* and drawing-rooms.

America is the paradise of women, and a paradise in which Eve is always victorious. But for men life is pleasanter in Europe than across the Atlantic, says the American painter in *Ève Victorieuse.* An American woman will excuse anything in a citizen of the Old World while she will forgive nothing in her own countrymen. American men profit from the severe discipline to which they are subjected by their womankind, if we may judge of them from Madame de Coulevain's novels. Her American men, splendid creatures, giants of fine physique, virile virtue, bright intelligence, and engaging candour, seem modelled on that fine specimen of humanity, the American President. These citizens of the New World contrast most favourably with the European aristocrats who in these novels marry American women—the French Marquis d'Anguilhon, the

Italian Marquis Verga, and Count Saint Anna. On the whole, Madame de Coulevain is in favour of these mixed marriages between American women and Europeans, at any rate as far as the women are concerned. As wife of a European, and mistress of a European home, an American woman acquires that tenderness and repose in which her sisters who marry in their own country are so conspicuously lacking. Madame de Coulevain has an old-fashioned belief in conjugal obedience. She regrets that it is not expected by the American husband, and thinks the American woman is all the better for having to render it to her European spouse.

Madame de Coulevain's two first novels, *Noblesse Américaine* and *Ève Victorieuse* deal chiefly with Americans. In her third novel, *Sur la Branche,* her compatriots play the most important parts ; but some pages of the journal —for in this form the book is written—are devoted to an English family and an English home. In the writer's last novel, *L'Île Inconnue*, the scene is laid entirely in England. The writer's object, so she tells us in the concluding paragraph of the book, is to introduce John Bull to Madame la France.

But unfortunately, Madame la France is too much of a home bird to care to make foreign acquaintances. It is but natural, therefore, that *L'Île Inconnue* should have received its most cordial welcome from the Unknown Island itself, which, if knowledge depends on a perusal of the pages of this volume, is likely to remain unknown across the Channel.

In *Sur la Branche* the writer of the journal, Jean Noël, tells of a visit paid to Simley Hall in Staffordshire, and sketches the character of an enlightened English squire, Sir William Randolph. In *L'Île Inconnue* Madame de Coulevain visits a humbler English home: Saint Olaf, the suburban residence of the Barings on Wimbledon Common. Her description of the peaceful life at Saint Olaf is a very faithful representation of upper middle class existence in a London suburb. Later she goes to stay at Claridge's hotel and mixes in a gayer, more frivolous society, composed largely of Anglo-Americans and English aristocrats. Meanwhile her Wimbledon friends, the Barings, have inherited a fortune and an estate. They leave their Wimbledon villa for the stately abode of Lofts Hall, near Bath, where Madame de Coulevain visits them in the last chapter of the book.

L'Île Inconnue suffers from being too long. It would gain by being cut down to at least half the size; and two hundred and fifty pages, instead of five hundred and ninety, would easily comprise all the real excellence of the volume, The book abounds in clever passages of acute racial psychology, interspersed, however, with some that are mere repetitions and others that are tedious.

On first setting foot on English soil Madame de Coulevain's impression is one of liberty and discipline, the two great pillars of England's strength. Her host of Saint Olaf is a pure Anglo-Saxon, very masculine, very awkward, and very correct. His imposing figure owes nothing to the tailor. He is not particularly pleased to welcome a French guest to his home; and while with mingled curiosity and anxiety he looks at her doubtfully over the roast beef, with true French tact she sets to work to fascinate him.

The servants are much better housed at Saint Olaf than they would be in a French home of similar standing.

While the Englishman prides himself on

having the monopoly of the home, the Frenchman accuses his neighbour of not understanding family life. According to Madame de Coulevain the Frenchman is nearest the truth. English family life lacks the expansiveness, the ardour, the zest of the French family circle. The members of the English family are cold and stiff one to another. Hence it is not unusual for an unmarried daughter in England, spending nearly all her time visiting from house to house, rarely to be at home. For the same reason hospitality crowds the house with guests, who are not required to be amusing; they are merely invited to swell the number and to render less perceptible that barrier of British reserve which in the privacy of family life isolates each member of the household. The English mania for hospitality proceeds also partly from that desire for constant change which is innate in every Britisher. He cannot remain long in one place any more than he can continue long in the same clothes. Hence in British homes there is constant going and coming, and *the week end* has become an institution. Every Saturday and Monday over the surface of the Unknown Island there is such a passing to and fro of persons in hansoms, railway trains, steamboats (and why does the author not add "motor cars"?) as would perplex an inhabitant of Mars or Jupiter come down to study the habits of earth-dwellers.

"While the Briton," writes Madame de Coulevain, "recreates himself by travel, hospitality, and eternal change, we recreate ourselves, so to speak, on the spot.

"Our Continental situation places us in immediate contact with the great currents of art and thought. Intuition, that divine faculty with which our race is endowed, often reveals to us what our eyes do not see and our ears do not hear. Everything tends to make us a sedentary nation.

"Our country, to which we are united in intimate communion, is bathed in sunlight and admirably varied. Nowhere else do we find those elements which most please us; and we stay in our native land and return to her constantly.

"Besides, in our homes, however humble they may be, there is gaiety, surprise, a fine exuberance of life. Free conversation on every subject imaginable creates a genial atmosphere which keeps us at home. We suffice for ourselves; hence our egoism and our exclusivism."

We are astonished to find Madame de Coulevain admonishing her compatriots to copy the English and live their lives in the open air. To many English visitors to France it appears as if the French excel us in that respect. At any rate, during the summer months they seem to take every opportunity of living out of doors. Wimbledon Common may be dotted over with the white dresses of nursemaids and babies and the red jerseys of golfers, but in the glades of the Bois de Boulogne and the Bois de Vincennes whole families are encamped. In Parisian streets and gardens the people eat and work out of doors. A Frenchwoman who does not possess a garden, or who does not live near a public park, will take her chair and do her sewing on her doorstep. In a French provincial town the present writer has seen two women seated at a street corner, hemming a sheet between them. The English housewife, far too shy to perform her domestic duties in such publicity, prefers to shut herself up in her own dwelling.

Possibly Madame de Coulevain is thinking

only of the English habit of daily exercise, but surely the French custom of living as much as possible in the open air is more beneficial than an hour or two's daily exercise out of doors.

Madame de Coulevain asserts with regret that among Saxons and in all Protestant countries animals are better treated than among Latins and Catholics. This is a sweeping statement; and we doubt whether it is strictly true, whether, for example, animals are better treated in Protestant Germany than in Catholic France. On the other hand, it must be admitted that in England they are much more humanely treated than in France, Italy, or Spain.

The English, writes Madame de Coulevain, invariably associate the French with the Pope. It would be more exact to say that recently they have *dis*sociated the French from the Sovereign Pontiff. The French, she continues, inevitably associate the English with the Bible. And here, we trust, there has been no dissociation. But the author of *L'Île Inconnue* fails to realise one of the great bonds uniting the English race to the Bible. She says nothing of that fine monument of English literature, the Authorised Version, by means of which the words and phrases of Scripture have entered into the very life and soul of the people. She fails to point out that France possesses no such classical translation. But may not this be one of the reasons why the Bible has exercised so much less influence in France than in this country?

The English Sunday, a byword abroad for boredom and dulness, Madame de Coulevain finds less sombre than it is painted. "It is less severe than we imagine," she writes. "Church is optional. The roast beef of Old England, flanked with Yorkshire pudding, is still the Sunday dish; and its all-pervading odour she calls *the Sunday smell.* But when the roast beef has been consumed in the middle of the day, tea, cakes, and callers are permitted in the afternoon. In certain Puritanical circles the day is more strictly observed: children are deprived of their playthings, and even letter-writing is forbidden. At the other extreme of Sunday observance is the Smart Set, who openly desecrate the Sabbath, play games, and practise the Continental Sunday.

Madame de Coulevain succeeds in completely taming her English host. She calls him *my dear boy;* and in the evening, in the library, while he smokes his pipe, and she is installed in the most comfortable arm-chair, they discuss English contemporary literature. Madame de Coulevain gives him a list of her favourite English novelists. Her tastes are broad, and this list is so eclectic as to include George Meredith and Marie Corelli—a breadth of eclecticism to which few English readers would aspire. In her earlier novel, *Sur la Branche*, the writer's tastes are more classical: Jean Noël's library consists of the Bible, Homer, Dante, Shakespeare, Molière, Diderot, *Don Quixote*, and *Manon Lescaut*.

Many passages of Madame de Coulevain's works have given offence in France. In *Sur la Branche*, Jean Noël had offended the French matron by suggesting that her daughters might be improved by being emancipated like English and American girls. In *L'Île Inconnue* Madame de Coulevain offends the French parent by condemning the upbringing of French children. On this subject the Frenchman is extremely sensitive. He adores children, and thinks he understands them. He is for ever inventing some new method of child culture; and he will never forgive Madame de Coulevain for saying that "nowhere is the human plant tended less scientifically than in France." Nevertheless, in spite of the numerous French systems of so-called *pueri-culture*, this accusation is perfectly true. No nation excels the French in drawing up codes of rules and inventing methods; none in practice is more prone to neglect them. The Englishman, in the first instance, acts without method, but he evolves his rules as he goes along, and, once having evolved them, he sticks to them like a limpet.

If the English child is brought up too much according to rule and too much in the nursery, French children are too frequently in the drawing-room, listening to conversations most unsuited to their tender years. While in a few rare English nurseries the discipline is too strict, as, for example, in one described in *Sur la Branche*, where a little boy of seven is condemned to sit still in the middle of the room, without any playthings, for ten minutes every day, that he may learn to keep quiet; in France children are subjected to no discipline at all. There are no nurseries in France, says Madame de Coulevain. This accusation, hotly contested by French people, while it is indeed too sweeping, is not entirely without foundation. It may be truly said that whereas the nursery is common in all English households of the upper and middle classes, it is a new and rare institution in France, only to be met with in the houses of rich people. Madame de Coulevain describes two English nurseries: one in *Sur la Branche*, at Simley Hall in Staffordshire, furnished with comfortable rocking-chairs of all sizes and a few simple playthings, its walls adorned with pictures of Robinson Crusoe, a map of the British Empire, and the inevitable text; another less pretentious, that of an artist's wife at Wimbledon in *L'Île Inconnue*, with its two curly-headed babies in white frocks and pink sashes, sitting in high chairs eating bread and milk, a picture suggestive of an advertisement for some patent food, which would have been truer to life had the babies been wearing holland overalls.

Madame de Coulevain, who is nothing if not fashionable, is a great bridge-player. Nothing, she maintains, reveals more clearly the fundamental characteristics of English and French than to observe them playing together at this game. "The Englishman plays with a mathematical strictness, and follows the rules as closely as possible; the Frenchman neglects them as far as he can. The Englishman deals stiffly and methodically, the Frenchman vivaciously, with an arm slightly curved. The Englishman holds his cards boldly, ready to meet whatever fortune may have in store for him; the Frenchman holds his hand more closely, arranges it slowly, possessed either by apprehension or by the desire to taste to the full that mystery of the unknown so delicious to the card-player. Throughout the game the Englishman is coldly calm and self-collected, the Frenchman nervously expectant. At cards, as in sport, the Englishman treats woman as his equal. He makes her no gallant concessions, and expects her to be perfectly straightforward. The Frenchman is always more or less affected by her presence. He plays less keenly, less correctly, when she takes part in the game, he allows himself to converse, tries to be funny, does not hesitate to distract her attention, and invariably holds her responsible when he is beaten."

In this clever portrayal of national psychology, Madame de Coulevain lays bare those fibres of the French and English temperaments which have distinguished them throughout the ages. Not only at cards, but in the more portentous game of war, we see the same characteristics revealed: in naval warfare, it will be remembered, the Frenchman always saved his ships, the Englishman risked his. While the Englishman is capable of regarding woman as a comrade, the Frenchman is always *le Grand Amoureux*. Woman plays a very important part in his life. "He is," says Madame de Coulevain, "above all things, the son of a woman. He loves woman's society partly because it suggests that affection with which his mother surrounded him in childhood and youth."

To the fundamental differences between the temperaments of the Englishman and the Frenchman, the Englishwoman and Frenchwoman, Madame de Coulevain devotes fifty pages full of piquant observations. Of French punctuality she writes: "With a Frenchman it is always the hour he wishes, not the hour that is." Of the British tendency to form clubs and sects, she remarks: "When five or six Britishers have an idea or a taste in common, they found a club to discuss it and smoke their pipes in its atmosphere. . . . So if some phrase of the Bible comes home to them with new conviction they build a chapel in its honour and found a new sect." Every member of an English club or a sect will naturally consider this assertion unjust. It may be too sweeping, but it is not without a germ of truth.

With great delicacy and tenderness Madame de Coulevain analyses the complex temperament of the average Englishwoman. Few French writers have shown themselves so sympathetic with a type of femininity which is essentially antipathetic to the Latin taste. In France, writes Madame de Coulevain, an Englishwoman is too often regarded merely as a person with yellow or red hair, spots on the face, prominent teeth, and big feet, whose chief amusements are climbing mountains and reading the Bible. The author of *L'Île Inconnue* realises that the soul of the Englishwoman is not so trim and so simple as it appears on the other side of the Channel. It is, on the contrary, extremely complex, idealist, religious, passionate, romantic, and yet mathematically precise, with a devotion to duty, a scorn of ease, an indefatigable perseverance, but with a certain pettiness and a vein of morbidity. This essentially British character is an implacable monitor: it kills a multitude of generous impulses, it confines the soul as in an iron cage; but it is necessary for the majority." I know no more searching and accurate analysis of the character of the average Englishwoman than that contained in this paragraph.

No description of English womanhood would be complete without a reference to femininism. To its consideration Madame de Coulevain devotes several pages, in which she regards it in a more friendly manner than in *Ève Victorieuse*, where she calls it a danger. In *L'Île Inconnue* she comes to the conclusion that the Anglo-Saxon woman is a born apostle. She has a genius for propaganda, which the last generation carried on by the distribution of tracts. The modern woman adopts more aggressive measures in her campaign "against alcoholism, uncleanliness, and vice in all its forms. If England is now the country where there are fewest deaths, if the public health has improved, if there is less crime, it is due to the increasing efforts of women." After such high praise, Madame de Coulevain's conversion to the femininist cause can no longer be doubted.

In *L'Île Inconnue* the three classes of English

society are passed under review, and compared with the corresponding classes in France. On the whole, these comparisons are just. But the writer is too hard on the Englishwoman of the lower middle class. It is true that she is not so good a housekeeper as the Frenchwoman in the same station, and that she, unlike her French sister, ignores the art of making much out of little. It is true also that she is more inclined to snobbery, that she aspires to having at-home days—hardly to *week-ends*, as Madame de Coulevain would have us believe. But her pettiness in such matters is compensated for by excellent Anglo-Saxon virtues of patience, perseverance, and industry, all of which Madame de Coulevain ignores.

In her domestic duties she does not receive from her husband the help that the French husband gladly renders his wife. And the wife of the clerk and the small tradesman in England has habitually to work very hard, for it must be remembered that she has generally more children to feed and clothe than the Frenchwoman of the same rank.

L'Île Inconnue, without being the writer's best book, contains some of her most brilliant writing. Its style, like that of her other works, is easy and fluent; but, owing no doubt to long residence abroad, some of her phrases have a foreign flavour. Her work suffers from being too bi-lingual. Some of the many English and American expressions introduced are not quite exact. For example, we frequently use the term *nonconformist*, but we do not speak of *conformists*. But such errors are mere trifles. Madame de Coulevain remains a keen observer of life, and her books full of interest for the student of humanity.

PAUL BOURGET

THE WORKS OF PAUL BOURGET

1875. La Vie Inquiète.
1878. Edel.
1882. Les Aveux.
1883. Essais de Psychologie Contemporaine.
Célébrités Contemporaines.
L'Irréparable.
1885. **Cruelle Enigme.**
1886. **Un Crime d'Amour.**
Nouveaux Essais de Psychologie Contemporaine.
1887. **Andre Cornélis.**
Mensonges.
1889. **Le Disciple.**
Etudes et Portraits.
Etudes Anglaises.
Pastels.
1890. **Un Cœur de Femme.**
1891. **Nouveaux Pastels.**
Physiologie de l'Amour Moderne.
Sensations d'Italie.
1892. **La Terre Promise.**
1893. **Cosmoplis.**
1893. **Un Scrupule.**
1894. **Steeple Chase.**
Un Saint.
1895. Discours de Réception à l'Académie Française. Outre-Mer.
1896. **Une Idylle Tragique.**
1897. **Recommencements.**
Voyageuses.
1898. **Complications Sentimentales.**
La Duchesse Bleue.
1900. Ecran
La Fantôme.
Un Homme d'Affaires.
1902. **Monique.**
L'Etape.
1903. **L'Eau Profonde.**
1904. **Un Divorce.**
1905. **Les deux Sœurs.**
Bonald.
1906. Etudes et Portraits—Sociologie et Littérature.
L'Emigré.

PAUL BOURGET, 1852

" La Tradition seule est grande, mes freres."—BOSSUET.

MONSIEUR BOURGET is the apostle of arrested development. Like Barrès, he is a traditionist, who would efface the work of two revolutions and return to those earlier institutions which hindered rather than encouraged the progress of society and individuals. " I write," he says, " in the light of two eternal truths—religion and monarchy." He is as firmly convinced as James I. of the interdependence of bishop and king. He who once admitted that he owes to travel all he knows, all he is worth, all he is, preaches that man is happiest and healthiest when he does not travel at all, when he lives and ends his life in the place and social rank in which he was born.

How Bourget came by such a doctrine, which is the negation of all progress, and how in his works he applies it to religion, politics, and society, is as interesting a psychological study as any with which he presents us in his novels. His own life until within the last ten years has been a complete denial of all those principles on which he has recently based his traditionalist philosophy. Born in 1852, his first fifteen years were passed in wandering with his parents from place to place: from Amiens to Strasbourg, from Strasbourg to Clermont-Ferrand, from Clermont to Paris. His father, Monsieur Justin Bourget, a professor of mathematics, had from the first destined his son for a scientific profession. And at the early age of seven it was Paul's ambition to write a great work on entomology. But as he grew older he wandered from the paternal path; and, much to his father's sorrow, a love of literature superseded science in his heart. Now he became as complete a *déraciné* as any youth in Barrès' novel of that name. He was one of that detestable species of the intellectually uprooted described in his last volume of Essays as "the curse of all our decadence."

In the early pages of his novel, *Le Disciple*, he paints a portrait of his own father in the person of Robert Greslou's father, who is a professor of mathematics at Clermont-Ferrand. His earliest memories, writes Robert in his confession, are of his father drawing enigmatical signs, geometrical or algebraical figures, in chalk on a blackboard, with that clearness of line which represented the essential orderliness of his nature, or writing as he stood before an architect's table, which he preferred to his desk, consisting simply of a large board of white wood placed upon two trestles. It is the study of Bourget *père* that the son is reproducing when he writes of "voluminous works on mathematics arranged precisely in the book-case, the cold countenances of scholars whose portraits engraved in copperplate under glass were the only objects of art with which the walls were decorated; the clock in the form of a globe, two astronomical maps hanging above the desk." These simple surroundings of the man of science are in strong contrast to those luxurious interiors which his son was later to describe with such minuteness in his novels of fashionable life. It is frequently noticed that sons more usually resemble their mothers than their fathers. This is certainly true of Bourget. Possibly he may have inherited from the professor of mathematics, who was a native of southern France, his fondness for abstract problems and a certain Latin craving for certainty which was to be an important factor in his intellectual evolution. But it is easier to detect in his nature tendencies inherited from his mother, who came from the eastern provinces. Certain of his maternal ancestors, who had from time to time lived in Alsace and Lorraine, were of Teutonic descent. From them Bourget received the romantic, mystic, sentimental elements which are the most striking features of his genius. The romantic strain in his temperament manifested itself early.

Among the few literary works to be found in his purely scientific home were two old volumes of a translation of Shakespeare, which, on account of their enormous bulk, were used at meal-times to raise the little Paul as he sat at table. But the old books soon became to the child something more than mere cushions. Their contents attracted his curiosity, and held his imagination spellbound by a charm never exercised by his father's scientific instruction. In these volumes Paul made his first acquaintance with life; as he perused their pages, the book became for him, as he called it in later life, "the great initiator." The Shakespeare of his childhood at Clermont-Ferrand inspired the young rhetorician of the Lycée Louis le Grand to find his chief delight in Homer, the Greek tragic poets, Lucretius, Virgil, Tacitus, and Seneca; while by Balzac, Stendhal, Musset, and Baudelaire he was being initiated into a more modern phase of humanity.

Meanwhile his scientific education was not altogether neglected. In 1871 he was walking the wards of the Hôtel Dieu at Paris. His hospital training exercised an important influence over his subsequent literary work. A doctor has recently written a volume entitled, "The Medical Idea in the Novels of Paul Bourget," to show how he conducts his psychological studies according to the methods of a biologist. Indeed, many of his analyses of character are suggestive of a medical diagnosis or an anatomical dissection.

In 1872, Bourget passed his licentiate; and in the following year, while visiting Italy and Greece, he had his first experience of foreign travel. On his return he carried out a project which had long been slumbering in his mind: he broke with the paternal traditions and with science, and embraced a literary career. This was a serious matter for him. It involved him in a breach with his family, and cut him off from receiving any financial help from his relatives. His uprooting was now complete.

While preparing for his literary labours, he solved the bread and cheese question by teaching in a private school, La Pension Lalarge, in the Rue Royer Collard, where the late Monsieur Ferdinand Brunetière was his colleague. The two professors had previously been schoolfellows at Louis le Grand, but had lost sight of each other during the war, in which Brunetière had served bravely as a private soldier. Brunetière, like Bourget, had disagreed with his family on the question of a literary career; like Bourget also, he had had recourse to teaching as a means of earning a living. In an article contributed to *Le Temps* shortly after Brunetière's death, Bourget writes: "I still see our mutual surprise, when on my arrival in the courtyard of the school, I ran up against my old schoolfellow. Our astonishment would have been still greater had we known that after being colleagues in that humble refuge for our young ambitions, we should one day sit side by side in the French Academy."

From the time of this meeting till Brunetière's death closed a friendship of thirty-five years' standing, the schoolfellows continued in close intimacy. It was Bourget who introduced his friend to the *Revue des Deux Mondes*, of which later he became the editor.

From 1873 to 1879 Bourget lived a laborious life, devoting the leisure left him after the performance of his scholastic duties to self-culture, the writing of verses, and of magazine articles. He was an occasional contributor to the *Revue des Deux Mondes*, and in 1873 there appeared in this paper his first literary criticism of note, an article entitled, "Le Roman Piétiste et le Roman Réaliste." He wrote also for *La Vie Littéraire*, *La République des Lettres*, and the *Globe*. In 1874 he published his first volume of poems, entitled, *La Vie Inquiète*, and, in 1877, *Edel*, a long romantic poem, overshadowed by a sombre pessimism, but revealing that power of dissecting character which was to be the chief feature of his novels. These were years of hard struggle and much burning of the midnight oil.

Writing in 1898, in the introduction to *L'Echéance*, one of his short stories, Bourget gives a vivid description of the heated intellectual atmosphere of those days. That was the time when Renan, our King Voltaire, as he was then called, was the sovereign arbiter of intellectual elegance. Those were the days of ardent battling for ideas and of universal curiosity.

"When the history of French thought in the nineteenth century comes to be written," writes Bourget, "one of the most difficult periods to depict will be that of the generation after the war of 1870. Never were there more contradictory intellectual influences than in those days. Young men just beginning life were confronted in the minds of their elders with those philosophical theories which had been elaborated during the Second Empire. M. Taine and M. Renan were the two most famous representatives of those doctrines. . . . Their basis was an absolute faith in science. Throughout the body of this doctrine there circulated the dogma of necessity. . . . Whether they wished it or not, their teaching resulted in complete fatalism. . . . In men of maturity it might be possible to conciliate such hypotheses with a respect for morality and with energy in action. For the young men of the day, such doctrines resolved themselves into principles of negation and pessimism." Readers of Barrès' *Déracinés* will remember that exactly the same intellectual surroundings are depicted in that novel. "The youths of France had arrived at this state of mind," continues Bourget, "just when the hour of national disaster had struck, just when the war and the Commune had imposed on our consciences the realisation of our duty to society and the necessity for useful and direct effort. The antithesis was too striking between the themes of the masters we most loved and admired, and the necessity for action which the misfortunes of our country, in spite of ourselves, laid upon our hearts."

Then Bourget goes on to tell how Taine himself realised this contradiction between the philosophy of the age and the national needs of the hour, how he sought to reconcile it in that gigantic work which, incomplete at his death, represented the labour of a quarter of a century, and remains the political breviary of every good Frenchman, *The Origins of Contemporary France.*

"In this gigantic work," says Bourget, "Taine endeavoured to reconcile faith with science, the civil world with psychology, the theories of his philosophy with national realities. But such problems were far beyond youths of twenty."

They beheld France deeply wounded. They

were inspired alike by the sight of her downfall and the hope of her speedy recovery. Under the impression of such a crisis they desired above all things to act. But their energies were paralysed by the fatalist doctrines of their philosophic leaders. "Our attempts were discouraged before we made them," writes Bourget. "The divorce between intelligence and feeling was complete."

Such is the picture that Bourget draws of the intellectual passions of the early seventies, when twenty years later he gazed down upon them from the mount of serene middle age. Then he marvelled at the mental and moral ardour of those days, and exclaimed superciliously: "Strange youth, whose greatest pleasure was the discussion of abstract ideas!"

Monsieur Bourget is thus constantly denying his past: an unusual rôle for a traditionist! But here we anticipate. Let us return to the strenuous days when he was teaching his class in the day-time, and studying life through the medium of books in the midnight watches.

It took some years before Bourget could find regular employment as a journalist. "Although my first study (that on Spinoza) appeared in 1872," he writes, "eight years later I knew not where to place my prose. It was not until 1880 that I contributed regularly to any paper." In that year he undertook the literary column of *Le Parlement*. In the following year he made the acquaintance of Madame Adam, and became a habitué of her salon, which, like its eighteenth century predecessors, was the nursery of the literary profession. Madame Adam threw open to Bourget the columns of *La Nouvelle Revue* she had lately founded; and here appeared those essays, collected later in a volume and entitled *Essais de Psychologie Contemporaine*, which first established Bourget's fame. They made a great impression on their first appearance, and have remained some of the author's most significant work.

In their discussion of the ideas of Baudelaire, Flaubert, Renan, Taine, and Stendhal, they present a striking *tableau* of the influences which formed the intellectual young Frenchman of the sixties and seventies of the last century. In his preface the author writes: "It has been my ambition to draw up a few notes which shall be useful to the historian of the moral life of the second half of the nineteenth century."

In 1885 Bourget published his first novel, *Cruelle Enigme*, which had been preceded in the previous year by a volume of short stories, with the title *L'Irréparable*. *Cruelle Enigme* is typical of the society novel which Bourget was to produce during the next seventeen years: analytical and discussing moral problems, but arriving at no definite solution.

The object of these books, as defined by the author in his dedication of *Cruelle Enigme* to Mr. Henry James, is "to give a personal impression of life." The personal impression Bourget succeeds in creating in these volumes is one of the corruption and decadence of society.

Cruelle Enigme, by no means the most powerful of Bourget's early works, strikes the key-note of his genius, and must therefore always interest students of his writings. It illustrates all his chief merits and defects: the plot is skilfully constructed, for Bourget is not one of those who disregard the warp and woof of the story: character is mercilessly analysed as if with that scalpel the writer had learnt to wield in the dissecting room of l'Hotel Dieu; femininity is vividly depicted in one of the writer's best portraits of women, that of

Madame de Sauve. On the other hand, the novel presents serious faults both of spirit and treatment. It is imbued with the most despairing pessimism. It reveals that disregard of the sanctity of marriage which, characterising all his early novels, has led serious critics to condemn these books as immoral. In treatment, the author's chief failing is that he analyses souls instead of creating them. Having begun his literary career as a critic, when he came to write novels he changed his *genre* but not his method. As in the books of his friend Mr. Henry James, the action of his stories is constantly being impeded by long analytical disquisitions, the keen insight into character, and the scientific method of which would be valuable in a treatise on psychology, but are completely out of place in a novel.

The main problem of *Cruelle Enigme,* stated in one of these passages of powerful character analysis, is how a woman who sincerely loves a man can in a moment of sensual aberration permit herself to become the mistress of another. This is the case of Madame de Sauve, who thus betrays her lover, Hubert Liauran. The passage in which the enigma is enunciated is so characteristic of the author's method that it may well be quoted here. It describes the emotions which succeed each other in Hubert's heart after he has discovered the treachery of his mistress:—

"Just as a man with jaundice sees everything yellow, so Hubert regarded the whole universe in the light of his disgust. There was not a single impression which was not tainted and sad. He rose, passed the morning among his books, opened but did not read them. He breakfasted, and his mother's presence, instead of touching his heart, only irritated him. He returned to his room and resumed the monotonous idleness of the morning.

"'After all,' he said to himself one morning, as he was getting up, 'I lived before I knew her! I have only to return to the state of mind I was in before the 12th of October. . . . I have had a bad dream, that is all. But first, I must destroy everything that would recall it to me.' He sat down before his desk, after having heaped more wood on the fire in order that there might be a fierce flame, and double locked the door. . . . He opened the drawer in which the treasure was hidden: it consisted of a black morocco leather box on which were interlaced the initials T. and H. . . . By the side of the box were lying two objects which Hubert had thrown there, the very evening of the day on which he had learnt his mistress's treachery: one was her ring, the other a fine gold chain from which was suspended a little key. . . . When he had raised the lid of the box he bent over it, leaning his head against his hand, and contemplated all that remained of his happiness, the trifles so insignificant to any one else, for him so full of deep meaning: an embroidered handkerchief, a glove, a veil, a bundle of letters, a packet of little blue telegrams, folded one within the other, forming a little book of tenderness. And the envelopes of the letters had been opened so carefully, the paper of the telegrams cut so precisely. The slightest details reminded Hubert of the loving reverence he had felt for everything coming from his mistress. Under the letters and the telegrams was her portrait. . . . She had had it taken for Hubert alone, and, when she gave it to him, she said: 'I was thinking of us whilst I was being taken. If you knew how this portrait loves you.'

. . . .

"As clearly as he knew from her own confession that this woman had deceived him, so he knew by these souvenirs that she had loved him, that she still loved him. For the first time since that fatal hour when she had confessed her fault, although it would have been so easy for her to lie, he allowed himself to utter a cry which he had never breathed in the days of his bitterest, most heart-rending sorrow: 'Then why! Oh why!'

. . . . . .

"Hubert began to think not only of his suffering but of its cause. To burn those letters, to tear up this portrait, to break and throw away the chain, the ring, to destroy these last memorials of his love, was as impossible as to plunge a sword into his mistress's quivering body. . . . He closed the drawer, incapable of enduring any longer the sight of these things which seemed made of his very heart's fibre. He threw himself on to a couch and plunged into the gulf of his reflections. Yes! Thérèse had loved him, she loved him still. There are tears, embraces, an ardour of soul which cannot lie. She loved him and she had betrayed him. But why, why? Possessed by what madness? Carried away by what intoxication? . . . Of what flesh was this deceiver that with all the appearance, with all the reality even of love, she was yet as unstable as water? . . . She smiles upon you, she weeps, and already she has noticed the passer-by, him to whom if he amuse her for an hour, with flaming eyes and smiling lips, she will sacrifice all your affection! Ah why? Oh why? Is there no truth in the world, if love itself be not true? . . . This new form of grief endured for days.

. . . . . .

"He had lived his early life in an unquestioning trust in appearances. He had believed in his mother. He had believed in God. He had believed in the sincerity of words and caresses. Above all he had believed in Thérèse de Sauve. Unconsciously he had assimilated her with the rest of his life. Everything around him seemed true, and Thérèse's love supremely true; and now by a mental revolution which was the result of a wrong education, this woman's lie identified itself with his life. His mother had brought him up in an unquestioning faith. This is probably the course most likely to convert the believer in everything into the denier of everything. . . . Under this misanthropic influence he committed the greatest of moral crimes; he even doubted his mother's affection. . . . He could no longer behold the beauty of humanity, he could see nothing but its vileness. And still he continued to cry: 'But why? Why?'

"This cruel enigma is partly solved when for the first time Hubert sees the man for whom his mistress had betrayed him. The nature of the man revealed itself at the first glance, and showed him the ambiguity of Thérèse's character. And then there dawned in his heart the saddest but also the noblest of sentiments he had experienced since his awakening, the only one worthy of his former self, the only one which enables man not to lose courage when deceived by woman: pity."

Besides the enigma of Madame de Sauve's nature, another is presented in the last pages of the novel by Hubert's weakness in returning to the Delilah who had wronged him. Indeed "life itself is a cruel enigma" is the last sentence in the book.

Bourget's first novel is utterly sad from beginning to end. It leaves a bitter taste in the mouth. Equally sad are its successors *Un Crime d'Amour*, *André Cornélis*, and above all, *Mensonges*.

The hero of this last novel, René Vinci, suffers something like the same disillusionment as Hubert Liauran. René is a young dramatist of twenty-five — Bourget's heroes are always between twenty and twenty-five— who has risen to fame by a startling success at La Comédie Française. He suddenly finds himself in request in the fashionable society of Paris. The contrast between his former obscurity and the brilliant circle into which he is now ushered dazzles and fascinates him. He falls passionately in love with an elegant beautiful woman, Madame Moraines, whom he meets at an evening reception. He believes her to be perfectly pure and true. In reality she is already deceiving her husband with an elderly lover. That lover's wealth supplies her with the luxurious environment which completes the charm already exercised by her beauty over the delicate, susceptible soul of the young René. Too late he discovers that he has been duped. By the treachery of one woman, René, like Hubert, is disgusted with existence. But more impulsive and less rational than Hubert, René attempts to take his own life. He fails, and it is suggested at the end of the novel that he will find consolation in mysticism.

These two young men are both led away by appearances. They have to learn the complexity of life. And in the learning they lose much of their early purity and nobility.

"Ah! if Bourget's hero," writes Anatole France, in *La Vie Littéraire*, "if the young poet René Vinci had re-read every morning in his little room in La Rue Coëtlogon, Chapter VIII. of the *Imitation*—if he had seized the profound meaning of these words: 'Flatter not the rich, neither do thou appear willingly before the great' . . . if he had sought joy in suffering and delight in self-sacrifice, he would not have suffered the bitterest of sorrows, the only sorrow which is really bad because it degrades and does not ennoble; and he would not have sought to die the death of the despairing."

In *Mensonges*, as in *Cruelle Enigme*, Bourget excels in the portraiture of women. Madame Moraines' portrait is as life-like as that of Madame de Sauve.

Following the method of his master, Taine, Bourget begins by describing Madame Moraines' origin:—

" She belonged, doubtless by heredity, for she was the daughter of a statesman, to that great race of creatures of action, whose dominant feature is, so to speak, the distributive faculty. Such persons have the power of employing to the full the present moment, while permitting neither the past nor the future to trouble their enjoyment. The argot of the present day has invented a very happy expression for this power of forgetting everything except the present moment—*couper le fil*, to cut the thread, they call it. Madame Moraines was an adept at cutting the thread. She had cleverly arranged her life ; she had a husband who was simple and in love with her, and an elderly lover, fashionable, egotistical but generous, who paid for the household luxuries. Between these two she made room for the young poet, who had inspired her with a passion at once sensual and sentimental. On the evening of their first meeting, René Vinci believed in the absolute purity of Suzannes Moraines : he doubted it still less when she became his mistress. She knew it ; but she loved lying ; she deceived him ; he was divinely happy.

" The lie of a woman one loves is a happiness as long as one believes in it. But one does not believe in it for long. In every lie, even in the most subtle, there are secret impossibilities which forbid its enduring. False words burst like soap bubbles. With all her knowledge, one thing Madame Moraines did not know, that one cannot deceive those who really love. They ask to be deceived, they would like it, and when she whom they love, through disdain, through cruelty, will no longer condescend to feign, they humbly beg the alms of one last lie. They say to her, 'For pity's sake deceive me, lie to me, so that I may still hope!' But even in the delirium of agony the unfortunate cannot escape from his fatal insight. René Vinci soon realised that he was deceived."

Such observations are cruelly true. These books are indeed sad, with a sadness more bitter than death.

Bourget's lengthy and minute descriptions of the elegant surroundings in which the scenes of his novels are laid have involved him in the charge of snobbery. "The Perfect Snob" was the title of a review of his last novel. Octave Mirbeau's Femme de Chambre is made to write in her journal that in M. Bourget's circle, in order to have a soul, you must possess at least a hundred thousand francs a year. The author of a recent book entitled *Les Grands Convertis*, with a minuteness worthy of Bourget himself, has collected some curious statistics. He reckons how many of Bourget's three hundred and ninety-one characters belong to the upper classes, and discovers that while one hundred and eleven bear titles or at least a *particule*, and seventy-six are of the high *bourgeoisie*, only three artisans and two peasants represent the working classes. Critics never tire of jeering at the infinite pains with which Bourget describes every object of his heroine's luxurious surroundings; her silver penholder engraved with her initial, her silken nightgown, her porcelain tea-cups, and her elegant brougham. "In this little boudoir on wheels," he tells us in a style that recalls Molière's *Précieuses*, "a hot-water bottle nestles at her feet, a mirror invites her glance, a pocket with note-book and visiting-cards reminds her of social duties, and a carriage clock marks the flight of delicious moments." Such passages, somewhat suggestive of the Tailor and Cutter's Young Man, proves that Bourget possesses what he himself calls *la Conscience de Tapissier*.

The critics, however, who see in Bourget nothing more than an Academician who is as great an authority on matters of dress as the first artist of the Rue de la Paix, miss the chief import of his work. Anatole France, whose critical acumen is never at fault, sets us an example in taking him more seriously. For France, Bourget, is above all things, a psychologist and a moralist. If Bourget, like Disraeli, considers that the labyrinth of the human soul may for him best be studied in the rich and leisured classes, he has a perfect right to choose his own subjects. Only in passing let us note that here again he breaks traditionist continuity. Himself belonging to the laborious professional class, according to his own traditionalism he would be more likely to conduct his psychological investigations with accuracy by turning his attention to such subjects as his birth and upbringing qualify him best to understand. That Bourget when he depicts the leisured rich does indeed mistake his rôle is proved on the few occasions on which he condescends to portray his equals.

The most powerful novel he has ever written, possibly the only one of his novels that will live, is *Le Disciple*. Here the two principal characters, Robert Greslou, the disciple, and Adrien Sixte, the master, belong to the writer's own professional class. One the son of a lycée professor, the other of a watchmaker, they have been brought up in the severest simplicity, but their natures are sufficiently complex to provide the novelist with material for the most profound of his psychological studies.

Throughout his literary career Bourget has retained something of the pedagogic manner of his early calling. After all he is ever the professor. The didactic habit persists in his custom of introducing his novels by prefaces, setting forth the objects of the works they introduce.

The preface of *Le Disciple* is an epoch-making production, at once a sermon and the manifesto of a new school. It is addressed to the youths of France, to whom Bourget appeals in Théodore de Banville's eloquent lines :—

> "Vous en qui je salue une nouvelle aurore
> Vous tous qui m'aimerez
> Jeunes hommes des temps qui ne sont pas encore
> O bataillons sacrés !"

These sacred battalions of the future are called upon to cultivate two great virtues—the power of loving, and the power of willing—and to beware of the hypercritical spirit. The evil of such a spirit leading Hubert Liauran to doubt even his mother's love the writer had already portrayed in *Cruelle Enigme.*

This preface is an apology for the psychological novel. In opposition to Realists, Bourget asserts the importance of the spiritual element as against the material in man's nature.

"Science of to-day," he writes, "science that is sincere and modest, recognises that beyond the limits of its analysis extends the domain of the unknowable. Old Littré, who was a saint, spoke eloquently of that ocean of mystery washing our very shores, but over the waters of which we have no barque to carry us. To those who tell you that beyond that ocean there is nothing but blackness and death, have the courage to reply, 'You do not know.' And, since you know, since you feel that there is a soul within you, strive that that soul may not die before your body. I swear to you, my child, that France requires you to think such thoughts, and may this book help you to think them."

There are two problems in *Le Disciple*—

one major, one minor. The major problem is that of a teacher's responsibility for the doctrines he teaches. Adrien Sixte has invented a system of determinist philosophy, propounded in three volumes, which fall into the hands of a brilliant young student, Robert Greslou, endowed with an acute but ill-balanced mind. Monsieur Sixte's theories acting on this young man's degenerate nature land him in prison, on the accusation of having murdered the daughter of the house, in which he was acting as tutor. How far is Adrien Sixte responsible for Robert Greslou's actions? This is the major problem of the novel.

Robert has not actually committed the murder. The girl had taken her own life. Morally, however, though not legally, Robert is as guilty of her death as if he had himself administered the poison which had caused it. The philosopher is aware of this. He knows all the details of the tragedy from the disciple's own confession written in prison and sent by him to the Master in a sealed packet, bearing on its envelope the injunction that the document is to be read only on condition of its contents being kept a profound secret.

With a strain of nobility by no means impossible in a nature otherwise depraved, Robert has undertaken to save the poor girl's honour, which he had compromised, by sacrificing his own life ; he will not deny the charge of murder. Here is the second problem of the novel : by breaking the seal of the packet and perusing its pages, the Master tacitly promised to observe his disciple's condition of secrecy. Ought he, however, by keeping this promise, to allow a man innocent in the eyes of the law to suffer death? He evades the problem rather than solves it. By an anonymous letter he forces the one other person aware of Robert's innocence, the dead girl's brother, to assert it in court and save Robert's life. The miscarriage of legal justice is thus averted, but moral justice asserts itself when Robert, on leaving the law court, falls a victim to the brother's vengeance.

The major problem of *Le Disciple*, the responsibility of Adrien Sixte for the crime of Robert Greslou, is discussed in pages of powerful analysis laying bare the workings of the philosopher's mind after he has perused his pupil's confession. The pages of the confession tell of a criminal aberration of soul related with a mingling of pride and shame, cynicism and candour, infamy and superiority. And behind it all the teacher hears the disciple's voice for ever proclaiming: "I have lived passionately and completely with your thoughts and on your thoughts." In vain he argues against his responsibility; he is bound, says Bourget, to admit that Robert Greslou, of a temperament naturally dangerous, had found in his, Sixte's, doctrines a soil for the development of his worst instincts. He fails, therefore, to exonerate himself from a certain responsibility in Greslou's crime. Such a conclusion is in direct contradiction to the Master's philosophy, which taught him to regard as absurd the idea that a teacher is responsible for the evil interpretation of his doctrine made by some decadent disciple. Adrien Sixte's solution of this moral problem is illogical. If every doctrine were to be tested by the application made of it by the Greslous of the world, surely none should stand. Greslou had in his confession admitted that in childhood he had sucked corruption from the purest and holiest influences. That admission should in itself have been sufficient to exonerate the philosopher from all responsibility. In the conclusion of *Le Disciple* Bourget reveals one of the characteristic weaknesses of his logic; he is too prone to prove all by one solitary and rare case, like the young man who said he always read divorce and criminal cases, as he liked to know how most other people usually lived.

Still, when all is said, *Le Disciple* remains the most vigorous of the author's works. Robert Greslou's confession, in the keenness of its analysis, is superior to anything of the kind in French literature. By the lucidity of his style Bourget drives home his arguments and never fails to carry the reader with him. As we read page after page we agree with his reasoning; it is only when we glance back on the work as a whole that we perceive the weakness of his logic.

The intense, even gruesome seriousness of *Le Disciple* is relieved by the character of Adrien Sixte's old housekeeper, Mademoiselle Mariette Trapenard. She is a devout Catholic, who, shocked by her master's paganism, hopes to convert him against his will by sewing into his garments medals blessed by the priest. Monsieur Sixte is far too absent-minded even to perceive the pious attentions of his servant.

The closing paragraph of *Le Disciple* reveals an accentuation of that mystic tendency which had already appeared in several of the author's earlier works.

Adrien Sixte, as he watches by the dead body of his pupil, realises the limitations of human knowledge ; a like realisation had come to Dorsenne in *Cosmopolis* and to René Vinci in *Mensonges.* In Bourget's first prose volume, *Les Essais de Psychologie*, occurs the sentence : "The hopeful hypothesis has as great a chance of being true as the despairing one." Balzac's famous dictum : "Religion alone can prepare, control, and direct thought, the principle of good and evil," occurs more than once in Bourget's early novels, and is an index of the writer's ultimate intellectual destination. Gradually his vague mysticism was shaping itself into a more definite religious belief. He was, in truth, drawing nearer to the Church, to which his ancestors had belonged for centuries and centuries. In the words of Jean Monneron in *L'Etape*, he could no longer live sundered from the dead (*sans mes morts*) ; he must return to the heart of France (*me replonger dans la plus profonde France*). Bourget endeavoured to correct the numerous breaks with tradition of his earlier years by returning to the faith of his fathers. The Abbé Taconnet in *Mensonges*, pointing to the crucifix, says: "None but He can explain the sufferings and passions of humanity. You will find no remedy elsewhere." This was the conclusion at which Bourget had arrived when, in 1902, he published *L'Etape*. "Valiantly, logically, irresistibly, the last novel of M. Paul Bourget proclaims the absolute adhesion of the master to the Catholic faith," wrote a Catholic critic [1] soon after the publication of this novel. His joining the Catholic Church Bourget himself described as an incident in his progress along the path of psychological investigation. There were others who hinted that the novelist's inspiration had shown signs of being played out. The late Monsieur Frommel, writing [2] three years before the publication of *L'Etape*, asks what will become of Monsieur Bourget? "His novels grow more and more alike. Exhausted imagination, dearth of ideas, hardness of heart are enemies threatening and too often overwhelming our

[1] M. Gilbert in *Etudes Littéraires France et Belgique*.

[2] *Etudes Littéraires et Morales*.

young writers. To triumph over them there must be something more than work and talent; that youthful vigour, that guiding impulse alone communicated to great minds by great hopes is necessary. It is not enough to be an artist. One must be also a man, and to be a man one must believe in something."

It is difficult to tell in what Monsieur Bourget did believe when he wrote his early works. Certainly not in humanity and hardly in God. A shadowy idea that in some dark limbo faith and science might possibly be reconciled; such was his nearest approach to religion. If so arid a faith could ever have been a spring of inspiration, it was a source which in 1889 was showing every sign of speedy permanent drought. Bourget of *Mensonges* was altarless and templeless. However he may object to the application of the term conversion to his case, there is every proof that between the publication of *Mensonges* and that of *L'Etape* he had passed through an intellectual crisis. The fact remains that the Bourget of *L'Etape* is miles asunder from the Bourget of *Mensonges*. The early Bourget, a painter of cynical, decadent young men, of heartless, faithless women, was in philosophy destructive and in morals a voluptuary. The later Bourget, a painter of idealists, simple-minded, pure-hearted men and virtuous women, is constructive in philosophy and strict in morals. Yet Bourget forbids us to speak of his conversion ; psychological evolution we are to call it. This evolution we see dimly foreshadowed in *Le Disciple.* In *L'Etape* it is complete. Here he appears a full-blown Catholic and monarchist ; in a word, a traditionist. Henceforth his creed is that of Bonald : one religion and one government, without which there can be no stability in this world and no salvation in the next. Religion is the necessary consequence of the fundamental laws of the family. In political society the three elements of the family find their corollary in the sovereign power, the minister and the subject ; in religion, in God, the Mediator and Man.

This cast-iron system of dogma is further enforced by the theory that a family in order to be healthy must continue amidst the material and moral surroundings of its origin, and that if it advance at all it must be only by gradual stages.

The ancient aristocratic institutions, therefore, because they hindered rather than encouraged the rise of the lower classes, were wiser than the present democracy, which the writer condemns as *L'Erreure Française*. Fully equipped with this very definite body of doctrine, Bourget proceeds to expound and illustrate it in *L'Etape*.

The family of Joseph Monneron, professor of rhetoric at the Lycée Louis le Grand, a peasant turned professor, by its threefold departure from the place of its origin, the God of its fathers and the social condition of its ancestors, illustrates *L'Erreure Française*; and the family disasters are represented as the inevitable consequences of the family break with tradition.

Never was there a more perfect instance of what the French call *un roman à thèse*. On every page of *L'Etape* the thesis is obvious. And yet the writer fails to prove his point. He fails to persuade the unprejudiced reader that the crime of Joseph Monneron's eldest son Antoine, the seduction of his daughter Julie, and the decadence of his youngest born Gaspard, result from the family's departure from the ancient ways.

The impartial reader is more likely to

attribute the Monnerons' misfortune to the father's unfortunate marriage with a scatter-brained, frivolous person totally unfitted to bring up a family. Bourget himself, in one passage of the novel, explicitly states that Antoine's crime and Gaspard's decadence are the results of their mother's unwise training. Julie's betrayer meanwhile is a member of that very nobility whom we are to regard as the salt of the earth. Bourget would have us believe that Monneron's unfortunate marriage is in itself the result of his departure from ancestral customs. Had he remained at home among his own relations, and in the rank of life in which he was born, a more suitable wife would have been found for him. But here Bourget enters the domain of the might-have-beens, about which it is impossible to argue.

The case against the so-called author of the family misfortunes and for traditionism is eloquently put by the professor's second son Jean in conversation with Monsieur Ferrand, a Catholic professor, whose daughter Jean wishes to marry. Jean is the only member of the family who turns out well; but then he realises *L'Erreure Française*, and seeks to correct it by becoming a Catholic. Ferrand

and Joseph Monneron had been schoolfellows and friends until their religious differences had separated them.

"You know him," says Jean, speaking of his father to Monsieur Ferrand. "You know how completely he is wrapped up in his thoughts, and, at the same time, how sensitive he is, almost violent, and for so many reasons. Distinguished as he is, there is much of the peasant in his nature."

It is curious to find a Christian writing so scornfully of the peasant. Has Monsieur Bourget forgotten the peasant apostles and peasant popes? One wonders what would have been the history of the Christian Church if such men had been traditionists, and refused to perform any but those duties marked out for them by their peasant origin.

Monneron's son continues: "His not having been accustomed to middle-class life in childhood is the cause of a violent temper, which I, with my excessive sensitiveness, have never been able to face. You know that, at the same time, he is so extreme an idealist that his idealism borders on eccentricity. Where could he have learnt to know life and to live it? What influences has he experienced? In his youth he was at school, where manners and instruction placed him out of touch with his family. At college he lived among his books and ideas. . . . He has never acquired that insight into character which you, my dear master, have derived from so many sources. You have had a family and a family circle. You have had a country, that Anjou which, as you have so often said, gives you so many points of contact with living realities. But his parents came from Quintenas, he studied at Tournon, he prepared for his examinations at Lyons, he married at Nice; my brother was born at Besançon, I at Nantes, my sister at Lille, my youngest brother at Versailles, we live at Paris. Do we belong to the Centre, the South, the East, the West? We do not know, neither does our father."

The writer's own biography suggests a startling parallel with the experiences just related. If a territorial basis be necessary for the formation of a healthy mind, what trust can be placed in Bourget's doctrines? His father, as we have seen, was a native of Ardèche, his mother of Alsace-Lorraine; he was born at Amiens, spent his early childhood at Strasbourg, went to school at Clermont, to college at Paris. Are his conclusions not just as likely to be false as those of Joseph Monneron? or would he argue that by returning to the religion of his ancestors he has corrected the influence of those territorial aberrations, at any rate, as far as his later writings are concerned?

But to return to Jean Monneron's analysis of the paternal temperament. There is a flavour of modernity in this patronising attitude assumed by the son towards his father which we should expect to find rather in the works of an advanced thinker like Mr. Bernard Shaw, than in those of a traditionist like Monsieur Bourget.

"His ideas are for him country, family, and reality," continues Jean. "How bitterly I used to realise when I was a boy that he did not really see me or my brothers and sister, that he only saw his own thoughts! But I did not then understand that this blindness was voluntary, although I do understand it now. He not only does not see life; he is determined not to see it, because its realities would be too painful. In politics he has always been a Republican, with what an ardent faith in the principles of '89 you know.

"In vain facts have shown him that the deeper France plunges into Jacobin parliamentarism, the more deadly grows her disease; he is determined to ignore it."

Jean goes on to give a graphic picture of the arduous life led by his father, who, to all but the prejudiced reader, must appear as a noble hero of modern democracy.

"His profession of government official, burdened with a family, has led him to undertake coaching, in order to be able to insure his life, so that his widow may live decently after his death. Since leaving college he has not had one year in which to write a book, and you know how he loves letters. His life has been passed in drudgery, and all for our sakes."

Monneron's patient self-sacrifice and devotion to duty compel even his patronising son to render this tribute to his virtue. But it is not Jean's usual manner of speaking of his father. In the tone of the perfect prig, he continues throughout the volume to criticise one whose shoe-latchet he is not worthy to unloose. Joseph Monneron, whom we are asked to regard as the destroyer of his family, is the noblest character Bourget has ever painted. His views represent that general outlook on life, which, as Catholicism decays, is forming itself in the minds of French thinkers. France's hope for the future lies not in Bourget's shibboleth of racial nobility, but in that very type of *intellectuel*, frequently of peasant origin, and fortunately by no means rare, whom Monneron represents. One fault Bourget attributes, and attributes justly, to Monneron, and to those who share his opinions: they are intolerant; their aim is to conquer liberty before they practise it. We are reminded of Bonald's startling sentence: "A supremely intelligent being must necessarily be intolerant." Unfortunately the saying applies equally to the supremely unintelligent.

As a study of intellectual life in contemporary France, interpreted from the Catholic point of view by one who knows also the other side, *L'Etape* is valuable, and none the less interesting, because it creates an entirely different impression from that intended by the author. The plot is artistically constructed; but here, as in all Bourget's novels, the action is frequently impeded by long pages of psychological analysis.

A story cleverly interwoven with the main theme is that of the Tolstoi Union, a kind of French University Settlement, founded by a group of *intellectuels*, of whom the most interesting is the Jew Crémieu-Dax. In the creation of this character Bourget adopts the same method he had employed in the portrayal of Joseph Monneron: high-minded and nobly virtuous, he is nevertheless a failure, because he is not an aristocrat and a Catholic. In establishing the Tolstoi Union on the basis of "Nature, Science, Progress, and Justice," Crémieu-Dax fails to accomplish any real social reform; "because," says Bourget, "every doctrine not as ancient as society must be erroneous."

Into his next novel, *Un Divorce*, Bourget introduces the same type of character with the same object. Albert Darras is a free-thinker who believes in that new ideal towards which France is slowly advancing. Throughout the novel Darras is represented as the opponent of that traditionalism towards which his wife Gabrielle is reverting. *Un Divorce* is therefore another *roman à thèse*. Like *L'Etape* it represents the bitter conflict in contemporary France between two rival schools of thought, two worlds, two civilisations. But whereas in *L'Etape* the conflict is being waged all along the line, in *Un Divorce* it is concentrated on one particular point of attack:

on the contradictory attitude of Church and State towards divorce. From this treatment of the subject *Un Divorce* acquires a dramatic intensity which was absent from *L'Etape*. Gabrielle, the heroine of the novel, has divorced a brutal and corrupt husband. When the story opens she has spent twelve years of happy married life with her second husband, Albert Darras, to whom she has borne one child, a daughter eleven years old. A Catholic by birth and education, under the influence of her agnostic husband Gabrielle had been content to leave religious matters on one side and had ceased to practise her religion. Her religious interests revive, however, when her daughter attains the age of her first communion. One of the conditions of Gabrielle's second marriage had been that the children should be brought up in the Catholic Faith. According to his promise, therefore, Darras permits his daughter to be prepared for her first communion. The mother accompanies her child to the communion classes and finds her former religious sentiments rekindled by the priest's instruction. Henceforth the peace and happiness of her home are destroyed. She wishes to communicate with her daughter ; the priest refuses to administer the Sacrament because she is living in a position which, though legalised by the civil, is condemned by the canon law. The alienation of Madame Darras from her husband, the numerous domestic troubles all arising, so the author would have us believe, from the first false step of marriage during her divorced husband's lifetime, are related at length in the pages of the novel. When her first husband dies, Gabrielle asks Albert to regularise their position in the eyes of the Church by solemnising a religious marriage. He refuses, not unreasonably, to make such an admission of an error of which he considers he has never been guilty. He will not thus cast a slur upon the happiness of their union and the lawfulness of their daughter's birth. As the result of his refusal Gabrielle leaves her home with her child. For days her distracted husband does not know where she is. Then a priest is employed as mediator : to avoid her husband's seizing his daughter and bringing her up in his own opinions, a compromise is arranged. The priest advises Madame Darras to return to her home ; and the deeply wronged and much forgiving husband consents to receive her back.

With this unsatisfactory and hollow reconciliation the story ends. There can be no prospect of any real happiness for people so widely sundered by difference of belief as Monsieur and Madame Darras. It is clear that peace and harmony have for ever departed from their home.

Here, as in *L'Etape*, Bourget fails to elicit our sympathy for what he considers the right side. We admire Albert Darras more than his wife Gabrielle, who is one of those weak women who must have a priest in their lives. Her action in bringing an outsider to mediate between herself and her husband cannot be too strongly condemned. It finally destroys the happiness of her home.

The love story of Lucien, the son of Gabrielle's first marriage, is skilfully interwoven with this, the main theme of the plot. The description of Berthe Planat, the medical student with whom Lucien is in love, is one of Bourget's most finished feminine portraits. Berthe is the only type of the modern professional woman we have met with in Bourget's novels. It is characteristic of the point of view of Latin Christianity that Madame Darras prefers to allow her son and his mistress to live together unmarried than to give her consent to his marriage with one who had had an irregular past. Another instance of Bourget's complete adoption of the ecclesiastical attitude towards life is the importance he attaches to the death-bed repentance of a profligate like Madame Darras's first husband. In this matter we agree with Monsieur Darras, who expresses his astonishment that his wife could seriously believe that the presence of a priest at a dying man's bedside could determine his fate in the next world.

In his last novel, *L'Emigré*, Bourget has abandoned the *roman à thèse* strictly so called. The object of this novel is not so much to combat any particular theory, or to prove any special thesis, as to raise an artistic monument to that nobility of race in which the author now worships the flower of French nationality.

In this novel there are really two *emigrés*, the old man the Marquis of Claviers-Grandchamp, who gives the title to the book, and Landri, his son, or at least who believes himself to be his son when the book opens.

The Marquis is the very personification of pride of race, of "family continuity in effort, energy, opulence, and domination." He is a conservative of the conservatives, a worshipper of the ecclesiastical and monarchical past, and a supercilious scorner of the republican and rational present.

Landri, the younger *emigré*, respects the past as it is personified in the Marquis. But when the book opens, he is on his own account prepared to practise certain of the new ideas; he condescends to serve in the republican army; in the service of the Republic he is willing to use his sword against the Church; he is desirous of marrying into the *bourgeoisie*, for he is in love with Valentine Olier, an officer's widow, unadorned by title or even *particule.* It is unnecessary to relate in full a story which has recently been frequently analysed in English periodicals. Suffice it to say that the chief interest of *L'Emigré* centres on the conflict in Landri's mind between two sets of ideas, between the old world and the new.

This conflict is presented with the author's usual psychological insight, but with none of the powerful intensity of the analysis of Hubert Liauran's emotions in Bourget's first novel.

L'Emigré, like all Bourget's novels, is actual. One of its most dramatic passages is where

Lieutenant Landri leads his men to take a church inventory, and then at the last moment cannot bring himself to give the command for the forcing of the church door. The novel closes with a pathetic picture of the old *emigré* standing alone watching Landri and his bride sailing away towards the New World. We may disagree with the author's belief that the salvation of France depends on the reinstatement in power of the hereditary caste *L'Emigré* represents; but we cannot fail to admit that in the Marquis de Claviers-Grandchamp he has created a heroic and sympathetic figure; and that in *L'Emigré* he succeeds where in the two previous novels he has failed—in exciting our admiration for his favourite character. As a work of art his last novel ranks higher than either *L'Etape* or *Un Divorce*.

No review of Bourget's works would be complete without a reference to his short stories, of which he has published several volumes. In this department of fiction he is a master. That he has a thorough understanding of the technique of the short story is proved by his preface to Balzac's *Contes Choisis*.[1] That he is a brilliant executant of

[1] French Classics published by Dent.

the art no reader of *Les Recommencements*, *Les Voyageuses*, or his last volume of tales, *Les Deux Sœurs*, can deny. Perhaps the finest short story he has ever written is *Une Confession* in *Les Recommencements*.

The Teutonic element in Bourget's nature reveals itself in the matter and manner of his novels: he is a writer without a smile: he frequently tends "to bear too hard upon things," as has been said of the Germans. Perhaps it is his Teutonic strain that has caused him to be widely read in England. A large number of his novels have been translated into English. His lucidity has won for him high praise from that master of style, Robert Louis Stevenson, who, in dedicating *Across the Plains* to Bourget, "Traveller and Student," wrote: "I may admire others with all my strength, it is with you I would choose to live."

MAURICE BARRÈS

THE WORKS OF MAURICE BARRÈS

1883. Anatole France.

1888. Sensations de Paris.
Sous l'Œil des Barbares.
Huit Jours chez Monsieur Renan.

1889. **Un Homme Libre.**

1891. **Le Jardin de Bérénice.**

1892. Toute Licence, sauf contre l'Amour.

1893. Contre les Etrangers.

1894. Une Journée Parlementaire. (Drama.)
Du Sang, de la Volupté et de la Mort.

1895. Assainissement et Fédéralisme. (Speech delivered at Bordeaux.)

1897. **Les Déracinés.**

1898. Un Rénovateur de l'Occultisme, Stanislas de Guaita, 1861–1868. (Souvenirs.)

1899. Un Amateur d'Ame.
Le Prisonnier.
La Patrie Française. La Terre et les Morts. (Lecture.)

1900. **L'Appel au Soldat.**
La Patrie Française. L'Alsace et la Lorraine. (Lecture.)

1901. Une Soirée dans le Silence et le Vent de la Mort.

1902. La Genèse d'une Œuvre.
Scènes et Doctrines du Nationalisme.

1903. **Leurs Figures.**
Pages Lorraines.
Amori et Dolori Sacrum.
Les Amitiés Françaises.

1904. Quelques Cadences.
Les Lézardes sur la Maison.
La Vierge Assassinée.
De Hegel aux Cantines du Nord.
Ce que j'ai vu à Rennes.

1905. **Au Service de l'Allemagne.**
Une Visite sur un Champ de Bataille.
Le Voyage de Sparte.

MAURICE BARRÈS, 1862

"Now the world is possessed of a certain big book, the biggest book on earth; that might, indeed, be called the Book of Earth; whose title is the Book of Egoism, and it is a book full of the world's wisdom."—GEORGE MEREDITH.

"The Child is father of the Man;
And I could wish my days to be
Bound each to each by natural piety."
—WORDSWORTH.

"OF the young men who since 1880 have entered the French literary world, Monsieur Maurice Barrès is certainly the most famous," writes his fellow-novelist, Paul Bourget. He is indeed with Anatole France the most original of living French writers and a master of style. But while France has all the serenity of a classicist, Barrès is afflicted with a Gothic twist, which, in the opinion of many, obscures his style, and warps his view of life and literature. Nevertheless, he is a great artist, a worshipper of "that beauty of the word, plastic and ideal, the taste of which has such a delicious savour." His novels claim to be a presentment of the intellectuality of the young France of to-day; they are certainly the reflections of the writer's own intellectual evolution, a faithful mirror reflecting his advance from the individualist isolation of *Sous l'Œil des Barbares* and *Un Homme Libre* to the collectivism of *Les Déracinés*, through the experimental stages of *Le Jardin de Bérénice* and *L'Ennemi des Lois*.

Curiosity directed by method is for Barrès, as for Renan, the most perfect of pleasures, "the source of the world which it is continually re-creating, the origin of science and of love."

Barrès was born in 1862, at Charmes-sur-Moselle. He is thus a native of Lorraine; and he has never forgotten it. In this No Man's Land of history, as in Poland, patriotism has been the ruling passion of the inhabitants. From the marshy meadows round Domremy, in the heart of Lorraine, came the Maid who for modern times is the embodiment of patriotism. A century later, only a few miles away, in the picturesque old town of Bar-le-Duc, was born Francis of Guise, who was destined to complete the work Joan had begun, and to drive the lingering British invader from his last possession on French soil. In later days Napoleon drew some of his bravest soldiers from the eastern uplands of Lorraine; and Marshal Oudinot and General Exelmans were born at Bar-le-Duc. In art as well as in war Lorraine has distinguished herself. Claude Gelée was born in a Lorraine village. Bastien Lepage was a native of the same province. The Lorrainer, Ligier Richier, the sculptor of the realistic skeleton in the Church at Bar-le-Duc, was a sixteenth century artist of world-wide renown. In literature the line of poets and prose writers proceeding from Lorraine is too long to enumerate here. Victor Hugo and Alfred de Musset had Lorraine blood in their veins. To-day there is a Renaissance of Lorraine which originated with the veteran writer André Theuriet, now no longer among us. But his mantle of patriotic *lyricism* has fallen on a group of distinguished writers, of whom Maurice Barrès is the most famous.

The province of Lorraine even to-day seems to preserve something of its ancient independence; for in politics and religion it differs from the rest of France. While Paris and many of the provinces grow more and more pacific, militarism reigns supreme in Lorraine. The cry for *La Revanche* is by no means silent. The nationalist movement of the last twenty years finds here its strongest supporters. While in the summer of 1907 the French Ministers at Paris were discussing resolutions to be brought before the Hague Conference, in an eastern town on the Lorraine border, the Society of Veterans was holding its annual meeting, and its president, a man of fine culture and wide learning, was calling upon his comrades to adopt as their motto *In Memoriam*, and to remember that France must never forget; when he spoke of the spirit of internationalism as an enemy to be combated, his words were received with frantic applause. While in many parts of France the churches are abandoned, in Lorraine they are well attended. Rich Catholics lavish their wealth upon ecclesiastical structures, and costly works of restoration are everywhere in progress. The discretionary powers permitted to local authorities by the Separation Law are used in favour of the Catholics. It was in this militarist and Catholic country that Barrès was born and bred.

From his eastern fatherland he derives the most fertile of his inspirations. "In the past of Lorraine," he writes, "we seek models whereon to regulate our lives. My intellect may be interested elsewhere, but my heart everywhere else *s'ennuie.*" His inner self, mercilessly analysed in his first three works, he calls *ma Lorraine intérieure.*

Barrès was a child of eight at the time of the war. "If I question my early years," he writes in *Les Amitiés Françaises*, "I behold a paroxysm of French tumult: under a blazing sun, trains loaded with soldiers—soldiers by thousands, perspiring, drunk, their uniforms unbuttoned—hastening to the frontier (July 1870), while the whole of my little town, men, women, and children, leaning against the gate of the station, offered them wine, coffee, beer, and more alcohol, crying 'to Berlin!' We acted for the best. And a few days later, in the rain, throughout an endless day of sadness and stupor, came the troops retreating on Châlons, cavalry and infantry pell-mell, and mud-bespattered soldiers insulting their officers, among whom a general was weeping (at least my young imagination persuaded me he was weeping), one immense filthy confusion. And then two days later still, at eight in the evening, in the shadow, amidst our silence, five hussars appeared on horseback, holding revolvers. They preceded the great wave of the conquerors. . . . After that, all Wagner and Nietzsche and their powerful administration, what is that to me? It is not a question as to where superiority lies. In my sixth year, my heart went out along the road to Mirecourt, with the shivering begging Zouaves and Turcs, whom thirty days earlier I had been sure were marching to glory."

His childhood's memories were to strengthen that nationalism of Barrès' later life and works which he approached through the individualist phase of his first three novels. "External facts and incidents, events that happen without being a pure psychological development, shock me in a novel or drama," writes Renan in his recently published notes. Barrès' early novels, *Sous l'Œil des Barbares*, *Un Homme Libre*, and *Le Jardin de Bérénice*, must have been to Renan novels after his own heart, for their interest is purely psychological, there are no external incidents. *Spiritual memoirs* their author calls them; the *Book of Egoism* would be an equally appropriate title.

"We have had the historical novel," writes Barrès in a preface to *Sous l'Œil des Barbares*, "and the novel of Parisian manners, why should not a generation disgusted with much, perhaps with everything, except with the play of ideas, try its hand at the metaphysical novel." And so he proceeds to essay it.

At a first glance it may appear that the collectivist nationalism at which Barrès has now arrived vetoes the individualism of these early works. But, as the author himself maintains, there has been no *volte-face* in his intellectual history. He has gone straight forward along the path of investigation which has led him, it is true, to explore "fresh woods and pastures new," but never to retrace his steps.

If there be any connection between the inner and the outer life, if a man's acts are the outcome of his thoughts, a close observer of Monsieur Barrès' career will think twice before he approves his system of self-culture; for it led him, when, in 1889, he was elected deputy for Nancy, to support the Boulangist cause, and when, in 1906, he was returned member for the first *arrondissement* of Paris, to oppose in the Chamber the rehabilitation of Alfred Dreyfus.

In his later works Barrès has attempted to justify the nationalism which led him to adopt that attitude. In the eyes of some he may have succeeded, to others his politics will appear of a piece with a certain perverseness of thought which reveals itself from time to time in his early novels. But in extenuation of his mental vagaries, one may always plead the excuse, that his irony must prevent him from being taken too seriously, and his use of allegory from being burdened with a literal interpretation.

To avoid such an interpretation, Barrès, in 1892, published by way of a preface to *Sous l'Œil des Barbares*, a key to these first three novels. Here he attempts to explain many of his obscurities, and his oriental manner of writing about women such a sentence, for example, as that in *Un Homme Libre:* "She was nothing to me but a precious plaything, a living knick-knack—a passing instinct whom I adored merely that I might humiliate myself." The women of these novels, he writes, are to be regarded as representing merely "the sentimental tendency in a young man of the present day."

The obscurity, of which this preface is a confession, is a serious blot on the author's work. He has set himself the double task of expounding a system of self-culture and producing a work of art; and sometimes he falls between two stools, marring the artistic effect of his work and veiling his meaning.

At the opening of *Sous l'Œil des Barbares*, Philip, the hero of this and the two following novels, is a young man of twenty who has just completed his course at a provincial lycée. The book tells of his five years' intellectual apprenticeship, served first in his native Lorraine, and later at Paris. Philip is a type, we are told, not uncommon in the France of to-day, and likely to be seen more frequently in the future. He suggests at once the melancholy egoism of Chateaubriand and Byron, and the philosophic curiosity of Goethe. Possessed by a *fin de siècle* scepticism, Philip cannot accept the old standards by which his ancestors regulated their lives; and he has no other, for he has lost faith in ethics, religion, and patriotism. In an ecstatic moment it is borne in upon him that the only life worth living is a life of self-knowledge. Therefore, to withdraw within the citadel of self, to pull up the drawbridge, let down the portcullis, and shut out the non-ego, the barbarians, becomes the object of his existence. Yet so closely do the barbarians hedge him in that only at rare intervals is it given him "to construct his personal view of the universe," to concentrate his attention upon that inner kingdom which, says the writer, is not of this world. Nevertheless, when those rare moments of spiritual exaltation do arrive, Philip is so richly endowed with the faculty of noting the slightest sensations while they are in progress, that not one quiver of his intellectual being ever passes unrecorded. The events of his outer life matter little. They are briefly summarised in so-called *concordances* prefixed to each chapter. Such intense self-concentration, and the spiritual ecstasy resulting therefrom, will inevitably remind readers of Gibbon of the directions given by the Abbot of Mount Athos for the mystic meditations of his monks. "When thou art alone in thy cell," says the ascetic teacher, "shut thy door, and seat thyself in a corner; raise thy mind above all things vain and transitory, recline thy beard and chin on thy breast; . . . and search the place of the heart, the seat of the soul." Persevering in this discipline day and night, "the soul discovers the place of the heart, and is involved in a mystic and ethereal light."

Philip is indeed a western representative of Indian fakirs and oriental monks; and to the sane, practical minds of the Occident his egoism appears as contemptible as did that of Christian ascetics to the historian of the eighteenth century. In Barrès' second novel, *Un Homme Libre*, which appeared in 1888, Philip pursues a series of experiments in self-culture. In company with a like-minded friend, Simon, we are to see him withdrawing from the world into the heart of his native Lorraine. And here it appears that Philip, though mystic and solitary, like the mediæval monks, unlike them is no ascetic. He is rich, for without money the imagination cannot develop, and there can be no *Homme Libre*, says Barrès. Philip is surrounded by every luxury that money can procure. With everything in their physical surroundings conducive to ease and comfort, he and Simon attempt to create a moral atmosphere conducive to contemplation. The *Imitation of Christ* and the works of Ignatius Loyola are their favourite books. Balzac's novels are excluded from their library as being too feverish, and likely to inspire the solitaries with a longing for that Parisian life they have renounced. These two intellectual voluptuaries prepare for the contemplative life by a régime of physical and spiritual drill, suggested, no doubt, by the discipline of the founders of the Society of Jesus, as set forth in the *Exercises* and *Directory* of Ignatius Loyola. They subject themselves to an examination, physical, mental, and moral. They consult a doctor. For Barrès, like his Jesuit master, never ignores the interdependence of physiological and psychological conditions. To be afflicted with any physical disorder would be as bad as possessing Victor Hugo's mental twist, says Simon. And to their intense relief he and his friend are pronounced physically sound. Their mental and spiritual self-examination occupies days of silent reflection. Then, in an evening organised with extreme artistic delicacy, the egoists make their mutual confession, and exhort each other to bear in mind the day when their ideas, emotions, and conceptions shall vanish. Meanwhile, however, they resolve to enjoy the present. In communion with the egoists of the past—Benjamin Constant, Sainte-Beuve, Marie Bashkirtseff—Philip fortifies his soul.

In a journey through Lorraine, observing the works of his ancestors, he descends to the foundations of his own being. He visits the ancient ducal capital, Bar-le-Duc. On the historic heights of Sion he realises the causes of the greatness and decadence of Lorraine.

That province, "once the most populous in Europe, gave promise of a high civilisation, produced a handful of heroes, then lost even the memory of her demolished greatness and her effaced genius." Philip trembles lest he, the child of his country, should fail in like manner.

In these descriptions of natural scenery, coloured by historical allusion and patriotic pride, Barrès is at his best. Like a true egoist, he is only appealed to, he tells us, by landscapes in which he himself plays a part. "Am I a curiosity hunter," he cries, "or a collector of knick-knacks that I should take an interest in objects with which I am not personally concerned!" His landscapes are invariably overshadowed by poetic melancholy. As a recent critic has written, they are in reality moods, "states of feeling."

Travelling over fields tilled by his forefathers, contemplating the masterpieces of Lorraine artists of the past, Philip drinks deep of their spirit. These warriors in the vanguard of Latin civilisation warring against Germanic ideas never forgot to look with longing and reverence towards the Italian cradle of their Latin culture.

Philip too turns his gaze towards Italy. After a few months he has wearied of his solitary existence and the "barren analysis of his own organisation." After all the ego cannot be entirely independent of the barbarians. It must select those most sympathetic as its models. So, in a Goethian spirit, Philip travels to Italy. But even there he is haunted by the spirit of morbid egoism. At Milan he fails to find satisfaction in the Old Masters because he reflects that their works were accomplished without his aid. Surely egoism can no further go! Not till he reaches Venice does his artistic soul know the great awakening. And here, doubtless, as in many other pages of these novels, Philip's experience is the writer's own. In his preface to *Sous l'Œil des Barbares*, Barrès writes:—

"Reflecting sometimes on what I have loved most in the world, I have thought that it was not even a man who flattered me or a woman who wept, but Venice, and albeit her pavements are unhealthy, the fever they gave is very precious, for it cleared my sight so that my psychic life mingled with the depths of my subconsciousness in one vast reservoir of delight. And with such acuteness did I follow my most confused sentiments that in them I was able to discern the future in process of formation. My life was decided at Venice, and it is from Venice that I might date these works."

And indeed the most beautiful descriptions Barrès has ever penned are those of Venice in *Un Homme Libre* and in his later essay, *La Mort de Venise*, contained in a volume entitled *Amori et Dolori Sacrum*. Here as always the human interest dominates. The beauty of the evening light, "*une tache immense et pâle . . . brillantée sur la mer, rosée sur les maisons*," seemed softened in order that Philip —delicate voluptuary!—might the more easily contemplate the instructive beauty of Venice.

Philip's Italian travel is the crowning though not the final experiment of the book; it completes his evolution into *Un Homme Libre*. In Lorraine he had learnt to control his nature, to be captain of his own soul. Venice taught him the art of assimilating from the works of others what was most conducive to his development.

In Barrès' third novel, *Le Jardin de Bérénice*, one of the most artistic of his works, the ego, in the person of Philip, is still with us. Now it is to be educated by the study of the soul of humanity. Even amid the mystic contemplation of *Sous l'Œil des Barbares*, Philip had realised that one must not love in word but in deed. In *Le Jardin de Bérénice* he, to some extent, gets back to actuality. He becomes candidate for the chamber, and is elected deputy. But this outer life plays only a secondary part in the book. It represents only, so the writer puts it, our temporary ego, *ce moi momentané que nous sommes*. It is the development of the inner life, the ideal ego after which we strive, *le moi idéal ou nous nous efforçons*, to which the electors had unconsciously contributed, that is recorded with the greatest detail. The barbarians, enemies of this inner life, are represented by Charles Martin, Philip's opponent in the election. The fair but sin-stained Bérénice is the instinct of the crowd. Her irreflective materialism is, in Barrès' fancy, closely related to the brute instincts of the animals in her garden and even to the geological evolution of the monotonous country of Aigues-Mortes, where she lives. These subtle influences combine to direct Philip's attention to that unconscious activity which is the common basis of all the past of the universe. In truth, as the author has himself admitted, this novel is Hartman's *Philosophy of the Unconscious* in action. It is an illustration of Renan's theory that the more the reason of man develops the more he thinks of the opposite pole; of the irrational, of repose in ignorance, of the woman who is nothing but a woman, of the creature of instinct whose acts are impelled by a conscience, which is obscure.

Abounding in fine descriptive passages, the book is poetically vague and philosophically subtle. In a letter, represented as having been written by Seneca to Lazarus, Nero is glorified as an egoist who makes no attempt to reconcile the life of contemplation with that of action. Indeed, the evolutions of the ego become so bewildering in this novel, that, at its close, the author finally lets its burden fall from his shoulders. The problems of his next novel are less complex and of wider interest.

In his *Ennemi des Lois*, which appeared in 1892, Barrès proceeds to a series of sociological inquiries. The Enemy of Laws, André Mattère, is a young man haunted by the problem of how to organise a generation which shall enjoy true freedom without crushing a single individual, even for the sake of the general good. And André comes to realise that this can only be when the individual finds his greatest happiness in the happiness of others. This is a tough problem for our egoist.

There are two female characters in this book: Claire Picard and a Russian Princess, Marina, who personify the two sides of human nature, one merely sensual, the other purely intellectual. Claire, *esprit Platon*, as the author calls her, was, in plain English, a book in petticoats. She was possessed, writes Barrès, by "that thirst for knowledge so characteristic of the young girls of our time, who all have *la passion des professeurs*. . . ." In this shy child the intelligence alone was as yet awake. Claire possessed less insight into life than the Princess Marina, André's mistress.

On his return from travelling in Italy with Marina, André marries Claire and abandons the Princess. He and his wife visit Germany to study the effect of German socialist doctrines on German sensibility. That is a problem indeed. They are disappointed to find German socialists occupied entirely with an economic revolution. German socialism appeals only to *le ventre*, says André, "Oh! for something which will change the hearts of men." "It is a state of mind, not laws, that the world demands—a mental not a material reformation."

Returning to Paris, tired of Claire's pure intellectuality, André receives her permission to go back to Marina; and in the end the three organise *un ménage à trois*, which would be scandalous were we not to understand that this book also is an allegory.

Five years after *L'Ennemi des Lois* Barrès published the novel by which perhaps he is most widely known, *Les Déracinés*. This title —"The Uprooted"—indicates the underlying idea of the work. In *L'Ennemi des Lois* the author, while emerging from the pure egoism of his earlier works, remained an individualist. In *Les Déracinés* he has renounced individualism for collectivism. But it is collectivism of a rare sort. It is closely allied to, if not depending upon, that curious principle, suggestions of which had appeared already in *Un Homme Libre* and *Le Jardin de Bérénice*: a principle which the writer designates as *le doctrine de mes Morts*. What this doctrine is and how Barrès arrived at it, how he passed from individualism to collectivism, he has described in one of the most suggestive and poetical of his essays, *Le deux Novembre en Lorraine*, in the volume entitled *Amori et Dolori Sacrum.*

His analysis of the ego has resulted first in his substitution of society for the individual, and secondly in his recognition that we are not, as we think, masters of our own thoughts. "They are the distant reaction of ancient physiological tendencies," he writes, "and our reason, that chained queen, causes us to plant our feet in the footsteps of our ancestors. . . . We are both the continuation and the continuity of our fathers and mothers. It is not enough to say that the dead think and speak in us; the whole line of descendants constitutes one single being. The ancestors of whom we are the continuation can only fully transmit to us the accumulated inheritance of their souls through the permanence of local influences. It is only by keeping before our eyes that same horizon which bounded their work, their happiness, and their decline, that we shall best comprehend what is lawful and unlawful. . . . Every act in disaccord with the spirit of our country and our ancestors is a lie which renders us ineffectual."

Collectivism, therefore, based upon traditionalism, these are the ideas underlying *Les Déracinés.* The novel traces the fortunes of seven young Lorrainers uprooted from their ancestral beliefs, from their customs, and from their country by the teaching at the Lycée of Nancy, of their professor, Monsieur Paul Bouteiller, another Déraciné. Bouteiller is an orphan, a *boursier* at the Ecole Normale, and "a pure product of pedagogy."

The character of the professor, who plays an important part through this novel and its sequels, *L'Appel au Soldat* and *Leurs Figures*, is a satire on anti-militarism. Barrès was now a member of the nationalist party. These three volumes are entitled *Novels of National Energy.* National energy, the author would have us believe, is threatened in France by the party system of government; and Bouteiller, first as Gambetta's spy, later as the paid agent, in the press and in the Chamber, of the Panama Company, stands for the party man as opposed to the patriot.

At Gambetta's call he leaves his adoring pupils at Nancy for a post in a Parisian Lycée.

And one and all, each member of Bouteiller's class, as he completes his Lycée course, stimulated by his professor's example and attracted by his personality, follow him to the capital.

These novels, though in the true romantic manner abounding in long digressions, psychological and sociological, contain much more incident than the author's earlier works. They present a vivid picture of political and intellectual Paris in the last twenty years of the nineteenth century. Their only drawback to English readers is that they assume a much more intimate knowledge of the details of French political life than most Englishmen can be expected to possess.

The seven youths whose adventures in the active and contemplative life are the subject of these books represent various classes of provincial society. Three of them, Sturel, Saint Phlin, and Roemerspacher, are young men of means, who can indefinitely prolong their studies before choosing a profession. Suret-Lefort has from his Lycée days been destined for the bar, where, before *Les Déracinés* closes, he has already become a brilliant figure. Renaudin, a *boursier* at the Lycée, on Bouteiller's recommendation and by the sacrifice of certain moral scruples, becomes a journalist on the staff of a well-known Paris newspaper, and develops into a journalist of the most unprincipled stamp. Racadot and Mouchefrin are the two scoundrels of the group. They have inherited no nobility of character from their ancestors. Mouchefrin, the son of an unsuccessful photographer, is penniless; Racadot, the grandson of a serf liberated in 1793, is kept very short of money by his old father, who is as avaricious as most French peasant proprietors.

Plunged into the vortex of Parisian Bohemianism, Mouchefrin and Racadot sink lower and lower in crime until Racadot's life is cut short by the guillotine, from which Mouchefrin only narrowly escapes through the silence of Sturel, who might have been a witness against him, and the powerful advocacy of Suret-Lefort.

But meanwhile much has to happen. Belonging to different classes of society and moving in different spheres of life, these young Lorrainers remain united by the bond of a common birthplace. By the faithful assiduity with which they seek each other's society, they prove that they are not entirely uprooted.

The young Nancy schoolfellows meet regularly at the Café Voltaire, or, in less prosperous days, in a Brasserie of the Boulevard St. Michel. True, the reckoning of Racadot and Mouchefrin has frequently to be paid by their compatriots; but not one of the more prosperous members of the group ever on that account dreams of dispensing with the company of these disreputable members of their society.

Sturel and Roemerspacher are the idealists of the circle. Undisturbed by the persistent bread and cheese question which troubles their friends, they seek to find some common motive for activity. Their imagination is fired and their collectivist desires stimulated by a conversation of Roemerspacher with Taine. The young Lorrainer has attracted the philosopher's notice by a brilliant newspaper article on his work. Taine visits him in his humble lodging, takes him for a walk, questions him concerning his manner of life, hears with deep interest of the group of young Lorrainers, and enjoins on them to cultivate the idea of sociability. The minute description here given of the great philosopher—of his appearance and mannerisms, all chronicled with the greatest care—brings the reader face to face with the bodily semblance as well as with the mental method of Monsieur Taine.

Obsessed by Taine's idea of sociability, which Roemerspacher has conveyed to him, Sturel invites the members of the group to meet him at Napoleon's tomb on the anniversary of the Emperor's death, the 5th of May.

Napoleon is the *Professor of Energy*. "The tomb of the Emperor for the Frenchman of twenty," writes Barrès, "is not a place of peace, the philosophic ditch where a poor body once so active lies crumbling away; it is the meeting-place of the energies we name audacity, will, appetite. . . . Level history, suppress Napoleon, and you annihilate the condensed imagination of a whole century."

This curious conference round the hero's tomb has a somewhat mock heroic result. While Sturel and Roemerspacher are hesitating as to the channel into which their energy shall be directed, Racadot and Mouchefrin are free from all such doubts. Always in search of self-aggrandisement, they seize the opportunity to propose the foundation of a newspaper. Racadot is entitled to a fortune left him by his mother, hitherto withheld by his miserly father. With this fortune, which he represents as much larger than it really is, he intends to found the paper. Members of group shall be unpaid contributors, Sturel the unpaid editor, and Mouchefrin the business manager, not unpaid.

Sturel and Roemerspacher, perhaps reflecting that Napoleon was no friend of newspapers, hesitate to give this very commonplace form to their romantic dreams of energy. But as no other practicable method occurs to them, they fall in with Racadot's scheme. So *La Vraie République* comes to be founded. As one might expect from the characters of its two promoters, the newspaper is quite unhampered by prejudices or principles. Nevertheless it does not succeed. Racadot's fortune of £1800 is soon exhausted. He is driven to solicit financial help from various political parties and commercial companies; a proceeding which, coming to Sturel's knowledge, causes him to resign his editorship. Even these methods do not long suffice. Racadot and Mouchefrin are to sink to a yet lower depth. For Racadot there were no little economies. He sells press theatre tickets; he sells reviewers' copies of books; and because second-hand booksellers give a better price for volumes uncut, reviewers for *La Vraie République* are requested to carefully separate the pages as they read and only to peep inside. At a public execution Racadot makes a hundred francs by the sale of two tickets permitting members of the press to approach the guillotine. And henceforth, adds the author with grim irony, the paper declared itself in favour of capital punishment.

Lower and lower sink the fortunes of *La Vraie République*, until, to keep it going, Racadot and Mouchefrin even descend to robbery and murder. A rich oriental adventuress, known to be decked with precious jewels, is decoyed into a lonely part of the Bois de Boulogne, and there murdered in the most brutal manner. Racadot is arrested. Mouchefrin for the moment escapes. But Sturel, who was driving home from Le Bois on the night of the murder, had seen the Eastern woman, once his own mistress, accompanied by his two compatriots. Sturel is deeply agitated by the problem as to whether he ought to place his information at the disposal of the Juge d'Instruction, and so procure his old schoolfellow's arrest, or whether friendship would demand his silence. Whilst tormented by this uncertainty, he witnesses the lying in state, beneath the Arc de Triomphe, of Victor Hugo's body. That spectacle, one of the most imposing France has ever witnessed, when the inhabitants of the great city passed in one long procession lasting for twenty-four hours, up the wonderful avenue of the Champs Elysées, to pay homage to the ashes of their departed hero, described with the gusto of a true Romanticist, recalls passages in *Les Misérables*. Far on into the night Sturel watches the surging crowd, including doubtless many individuals low and base, yet as a whole animated by one noble, generous impulse. It brings home to him the solidarity of mankind, the idea so forcibly presented by Hugo in his works, the sacrifice of millions of beings in order that nature may produce greatness. Who knows? Perhaps after all, reflects Sturel, Mouchefrin's and Racadot's squalid lives were necessary to the great scheme of things. He must accept their destiny as he must accept his own. He will keep silence; and Mouchefrin shall live.

With Racadot's execution the story of *Les Déracinés* really ends, but the writer adds a chapter in order that he may chastise with another stroke of the satiric lash his butt, Bouteiller.

The Professor, aided by the eloquence of Suret-Lefort, and by dubious electioneering trickery, is elected deputy for Nancy. Although he has long since renounced pedagogy, the vestiges of his old calling cling to Bouteiller. In a public speech, after his election, he thanks the brilliant young advocate for his support, praising his talent, and, above all, his freedom from any taint of a Lorraine accent.

In form *Les Déracinés* is inferior to the author's earlier work. It lacks the artistic harmony of *Le Jardin de Bérénice*. Its unity is broken by long digressions. The classic finish of *Sous l'Œil des Barbares* and *Un Homme Libre* gives place to a style verging on journalese. In subject and treatment, however, the book possesses merits absent from previous novels: it is more human than anything Barrès had yet written; by the problems it poses, and the ideas it suggests, it is deeply significant; its sociological theories have given rise to the formation of a new literary school, that of *regionalism*, which includes many of the most brilliant writers of young France.

In 1900, three years after *Les Déracinés*, appeared its sequel *L'Appel au Soldat*. The soldier of this novel is Boulanger. In these pages we meet with the young Lorrainers of the previous volume, Sturel, Suret-Lefort, and Renaudin whirling on the giddy wheel of the abortive Boulangist Revolution. Mouchefrin appropriately re-appears, first as *agent provocateur*, then as political blackmailer, and finally as Boulangist deputy. Meanwhile the conservative and traditional Saint-Phlin and the philosophic student of history, Roemerspacher, look on with critical but not unsympathetic eyes; and Bouteiller, the Professor turned deputy, opposes the movement with all the bitterness of his pedagogic soul.

It required boldness to write the history of Boulangism within ten years of its collapse, when many of its principal actors were still living. But Barrès has never been found deficient in literary courage. As a member of the Boulangist party, elected deputy at the height of the crisis, he knows much of the inner workings of the episode. It is inevitable that he should write in the spirit of a partisan; but he is one of those rare partisans who realises the limitations of his hero and the mistakes of his party. "Boulangism is for him," he writes, "an incident in the series of efforts made by a nation disfigured by foreign intrigues to find her true greatness." Nevertheless for Barrès, as for many of his countrymen in the late eighties, Boulanger remains a hero. And indeed, even his adversaries will agree with Barrès that the General, the only possible dictator France has produced since Sedan, had much in common with those national heroes whom from time to time down the centuries she has passionately adored. He was of the same theatrical, slightly vulgar type, as Francis I., Henry IV., La Fayette. Like them he was animated by the great national passion for glory, equality, and authority. His dominant characteristics, according to Barrès, were a strong will and a kind heart. What was most striking in his manner was courtesy and *savoir faire.* His personal charm was enhanced by the frank glance of his blue eyes and the quiet dignity of his bearing. Barrès gives him credit for perfect disinterestedness. He more than once compares him, without saying exactly why, with Lord Randolph Churchill. In the opinion of the author of *L'Appel au Soldat* the strength of Boulangism lay in its placing the interests of France above those of party, its weakness in that it was the fever of a nation and not its conscience.

The career of *Le Général du Café Concert* is related with all the simplicity of a dramatic romance. Characters still to the fore in French politics, such as Clémenceau and Rochefort, appear upon the scene. And the book abounds in those glowing pictures which the author, in the previous novel, has shown himself capable of so vividly depicting: the General's departure for Clermont turbulently contested by the adoring Paris mob who refused to be deprived of their hero; the suppers at Laguerre's; the brilliant receptions in the aristocratic drawing-rooms of Paris after Boulanger had left the army; his duel; the mysterious influence of his mistress, Madame de Bonnemains; his followers' fears lest he should be arrested; his sudden disappearance from Paris, and his more sudden return a few hours later; his final departure for Brussels; his defeat at the polls and the disappointment of all his hopes.

While many may resent the halo of romantic glory with which Barrès surrounds his hero in his triumphant days, few can fail to be moved to pity by the picture of the fallen idol in the dreariness of exile. At London, in his lodging in Portland Place, in the Island of Jersey, at Brussels, we see him abandoned by his followers, tortured by the painful illness of her whom he loved most dearly, and then, when his fortunes had reached their lowest ebb, separated from her by death. This chapter in his hero's story Barrès relates with a tender delicacy rare in his treatment of the relationship between men and women.

Those who have at heart the peace of Europe must have rejoiced at Boulanger's discomfiture, and have found it difficult to mourn over his romantic suicide by the grave of Marguerite de Bonnemains. His attempted revolution is too recent for impartial judgment. But, when Time shall have cooled the passions of party, it seems probable that *L'Appel au Soldat* will be appreciated as a brilliant record of a political career, the last quivering perhaps of that revolutionary fever which, having accomplished much for France and for the progress of civilisation, was yet an ever remaining menace to the peace of the world.

But the author of *L'Appel au Soldat* is no advocate of peace. He looks for the restoration of *greater France* not only morally but geographically. The book is animated by a strong anti-Germanic feeling. Saint-Phlin and Sturel make a pilgrimage to the conquered city of Metz, and are inspired with an intense longing for *La Revanche*. They are infuriated by the German arrogance which, close by the tombs of French soldiers slain in the war, proclaims: "God was with us." "They inscribe God as their ally," writes Barrès in an outburst of patriotic hatred, "banishing our Christians from the Paradise of Christ's children, robbing our atheists of their share as authors in the civilising work of humanity, repulsing our soldiers as brigands, proscribing French thought as harmful. . . . She (Germany) excommunicates us; she preaches the annihilation of our language and of our ideas. It is a holy war. On the territory of Metz and Strasbourg, Germany, more cruel than those orientals who cut down olive trees and filled up wells, tends to translate her principles into deeds. She suppresses French thoughts in the minds of our children. As a living spring may be hidden beneath faggots, she attempts to conceal beneath German words a sensibility which for centuries nourished the race, and which the children had received from their fathers."

"Forget all the master teaches you," says an inhabitant of a neighbouring village to his child coming from a German school. "Nothing is true which is not in French."

In 1903 Barrès published the third and last novel of National Energy, a volume entitled *Leurs Figures.* Here he narrates the political crisis of the early nineties, which came to a head in the *Affaire Panama.* The book is written in a bitter partisan spirit. It enters in great detail into all the party controversies of the hour, and to English readers is even more difficult of comprehension than the preceding volumes. *Leurs Figures* affords a striking illustration of how Barrès' political ardour has marred his literary art.

At the same time his literary works have frequently stood him in evil stead when posing as a candidate for the Chamber. When, in the spring of 1906, he was standing as Nationalist candidate for the first *arrondissement* of Paris, passages from his novels reflecting on national institutions were quoted against him in a local paper. In *Sous l'Œil des Barbares* he had described Paris as "an ocean of meanness," "a plain on which encamp the barbarians"; he had written of the atrocities formerly committed by the French in Lorraine; but worse than all, he had said that the French army, instead of being a school of social morality, only inculcated lessons of drunkenness and debauchery. It was unpleasant for a political candidate to be confronted with such extracts from his novels; and it says much for the strength of nationalism in the first *arrondissement* that, notwithstanding, Barrès was elected. Although his politics are always creeping in to disfigure his literary work, he has never made any great mark in the political world, and seldom raises his voice in the Chamber.

On the 26th of January 1906 he was elected member of the French Academy, in succession to Joseph Maria de Heredia. Even into that serene atmosphere, Barrès insisted on introducing the strife of party politics, and on making his discourse a plea for nationalism.

His next political novel, *Au Service de l'Allemagne*, although something of a political pamphlet, is, on the whole, a more artistic work than *Leurs Figures*. The story of a young Alsatian's service in the German army is introduced by a charming description of the Vosges mountain, Sainte Odille, which dominates the Alsatian plain.

In *Les Amitiés Françaises*, which appeared in the same year as *Leurs Figures*, Barrès struck a new note. This book, the author tells us, is written for his son, Philip the Second. "It is a series of notes on a little Lorrainer's acquisition of sentiments which impart a value to life." Little Philip is three years old when the book opens, and six when it closes. He receives his first impression of the infinitude of the universe when his ball rolls into a hole near the hotel where he is staying. Henceforth friends from whom he is separated, playthings that he has lost, have alike all fallen into the hole.

There is no more delightfully humorous passage in the whole of the author's works than the chapter in this book describing Philip's affection for his dog and his quarrel with his German governess, who would not believe that dogs have souls. One afternoon, long before the hour fixed for their return from a walk, Fräulein and Philip, heated and both talking at once, burst in upon Philip's father. "It is because of Simon," says Philip. "Fräulein maintains that dogs have no souls." "Sir, you understand: it is a matter I can't explain. I know I ought not to annoy the child; but animals have no souls," says Fräulein.

"There, you see!" cried Philip, pointing at her as if she were a heretic, while the poor young lady, quite innocent in this catastrophe, seemed to say: "I understand, sir, that you do allow souls to animals: I foresee that I shall return to my great Germany, but my conscience is at stake!"

"I should have liked to steal away," says the perplexed father, but Philip pressed his point.

"Did you not tell me that a dog had a soul?"

Philip's father was obliged to agree; he tried to save the situation by a distinction: "It depends upon climate!"

"Ah! so it depends upon climate," repeated Philip, his honest eyes full of distress. "But, Simon? Are you sure he has a soul? there, you see, Fräulein." But though the immediate point of issue is for the moment settled, other doubts arise in the child's mind.

The quarrel revives. The sensitive Fräulein packs her boxes and is on the eve of departure. "I have nothing to say against the house," she, explains, "and the little boy is sweet; but on the subject of dogs' souls he is inexorable . . . and I should never have believed it possible to suffer so much all on account of a poodle."

To pacify Fräulein, Philip's father has to employ somewhat subtle reasoning. He explains that the child as a Roman Catholic has to be brought up in the doctrines of the Church; that the Christian Fathers, notably St. Thomas Aquinas, did not deny that animals have souls. In the end the irate Teuton is induced to unpack her boxes. Philip promises to refrain from discussing this tender subject with his governess. With his father, however, the matter is not allowed to rest. The question of climate worries him. And in the end he arrives at the conclusion that soullessness characterises German people as well as German dogs: a theory which his father does not correct. Thus the young Philip is educated in racial antagonism.

He is brought up to hate the Prussians, to believe that his *raison d'être* is *La Revanche*, and that when he grows to manhood Metz and Strasbourg will return to France. His nationalism is strengthened by pictures of Joan of Arc and Napoleon, by visits to the military manœuvres, to mediæval châteaux, and to Joan of Arc's home at Domremy. Barrès, with Huxley, believes that children should be brought up in the mythology of their country. Philip is taught to reverence all that is venerable, and taken to Lourdes. What he learns there it is difficult to discover. His father finds much to inspire those romantic reveries in which he delights. But the child refused to be edified by the picture of Bernadette, a little girl to whom the Virgin appeared. "No, no," cried the boy, "she is too young." He knew that the Holy Virgin lived long before Napoleon, and he had never met any one old enough to have seen him, therefore how could he believe that a little girl had seen the Virgin!

Such a book as *Les Amitiés Françaises*, with its respect for the ancient ways, and for many of the institutions of the Catholic Church, pleases Catholics, and has inspired the prophecy that Barrès will ere long return to the faith of his ancestors. The logical outcome of his traditionalism would involve such a return; and he has written, "Happy is he who, when all is lost, knows the way to the ancient altars." At present, however, he maintains his belief that life is meaningless, but that our part in it is to submit to all illusions, while clearly realising them to be such. To conquer in life, and triumph over despair, one must systematise the culture of one's thoughts and sentiments, had been the theme of *Un Homme Libre;* it is also that of *Les Amitiés Françaises.*

The idea of woman in this later book is nobler than in Barrès' earlier works, where she is simply regarded as a sex. Here in the tribute paid to Joan of Arc's purity, and to woman's ennobling influence on child life, she is placed on a higher plane.

Besides the two groups of novels we have discussed, and many pamphlets and prefaces, literary, political, and philosophical, Barrès has written three volumes of short sketches: *Du Sang, de la Volupté et de la Mort*, published in 1894; *Amori et Dolori Sacrum*, 1903; and his last book, *Le Voyage de Sparte*, 1905. These volumes relate the impressions produced by the cities of Italy, Spain, and Greece on the romantic spirit of the author. Throughout his wanderings his heart ever turns to Lorraine. "Venice, Sienna, Cordova, Toledo," he cries, "you know how ardently I embraced you;

but what did I find in you that touched my soul?" The supreme lesson that Athens teaches him is to return to Lorraine, and on his native soil to strive after Greek culture.

Le Voyage de Sparte, a work of high artistic merit, is the story of a Romanticist in Greece, and is thus an epitome of the author's work. We have traced him through varying moods and phases, from extreme egoism to that nationalist altruism which approaches the negation of the ego. But in one respect he has remained throughout the same. From the first line of *Sous l'Œil des Barbares* to the last of *Le Voyage de Sparte*, he is in spirit a complete Romanticist.

In common with Chateaubriand, the great founder of Romanticism, he sounds the loud personal note. He shares with him also a sentimental veneration for the institutions of the Church. But, Romanticist in spirit, unlike Chateaubriand, Barrès is classical in form. When his style is at its best, the melody and restraint of his clear-cut phrase is severely classical. In his blending of romantic and classical influences, as well as in the originality of his thought, he stands alone among living French writers.

RENÉ BAZIN

THE WORKS OF RENÉ BAZIN

1884. **Stéphanette.**
1886. **Ma Tante Giron.**
1888. **Une Tache d'Encre.**
1890. **Les Noëllet.**
1891. **A l'Aventure.**
1892. **La Sarcelle Bleue.**
1893. **Madame Corentine.**
Sicile.
1894. **Humble Amour.**
Les Italiens d'Aujourd'hui.
1895. Terre d'Espagne.
1896. En Province.
1897. **De Toute son Âme.**
1898. **Contes de Bonne Perrette.**
1899. **La Terre qui Meurt.**
Croquis de France et Orient.
1901. **Le Guide de l'Empereur.**
Les Oberlé.
L'Enseigne de Vaisseau Paul Henry.
1902. **Donatienne.**
1903. **Récits de la Plaine et de la Montagne.**
1905. Le Duc de Nemours.
L'Isolée.
1906. Questions Littéraires et Sociales.
1907. **Le Blé qui Lève.**

RENÉ BAZIN, 1853

"Of truth, of grandeur, beauty, love and hope
And melancholy fear subdued by faith,
Of blessed consolations in distress."

"A lover of the meadows and the woods,
And mountains; and of all that we behold
From this green earth."

—WORDSWORTH.

BY his delicacy of taste, elevation of mind, and charm of style, Monsieur Bazin recommends himself to English readers. Three of his novels have been translated into English,[1] and recently he has been the subject of articles in two of our quarterlies.[2]

His novels are a protest against those realistic methods in vogue in French fiction, in the eighties, when he first began to write. He considers the great faults of the realists to be a certain brutality, a tendency to attri-

[1] *Un Tache d'Encre*, by Quiller Couch and P. M. Francke, and *La Terre qui Meurt*, under the title of *The Autumn Glory, or the Toilers of the Field*, by Mrs. Ellen Waugh.

[2] *Dublin Review*, January: "An Apologist for French Catholics," by Reginald Balfour. *Edinburgh Review*, April: "Peasant Studies in French Literature."

bute too much to instinct, to dwell on what one of them calls "the sublime beauty of the ugly." Bazin accuses them of giving a wrong idea of French society, of ignoring or misrepresenting a whole class of environments and personages. Nowhere, he considers, have they gone further astray than in their description of peasant life, where it seems their aim to reveal all that is hideous in human nature. Bazin is ever intent on discovering the good which exists side by side with the evil. For him the strength of the French nation resides in that France which "in silence sows and reaps," and in "its reserve of obscure, laborious, believing, devout family life."

> "The lowly train in life's sequester'd scene,
> The native feelings strong, the guileless ways"

are his favourite subjects. He turns aside from "noisy, greedy Paris." He does not share that passion so common among French men of letters, from Molière downwards, for disparaging provincial life. It has too often, he says, been the custom to laugh at provincials for the amusement of Parisians. It is true that certain great writers of the nineteenth century have attempted to correct this in their pictures of the peasant. But Georges Sand's peasant idylls are "a compromise between veracity and sentimentalism." Balzac describes peasants in the light of Parisian drawing-rooms, Flaubert and Maupassant in that of a misanthropic temperament which filled them with scorn for all their fellow-creatures. Bazin, on the contrary, is overflowing with the milk of human kindness. He treats the artisan and the peasant with an exquisite tenderness. Moreover, he is a Catholic, and he regards poverty from the Catholic point of view, as a blessing in disguise. Such a doctrine may be economically pernicious, artistically it lends a charm and a rarity to his writings.

Bazin is well qualified to write of provincial France, for in the provinces he has passed his life. He is a *raciné* who must delight the heart of Maurice Barrès. An Angevin by birth, Bazin remains still in his native Anjou. Born in the country, near Segré, in 1853, he is now Professor of Law in the neighbouring Catholic University of Angers. His winters he spends in Paris; but in the spring he returns to the country, and stays there till the end of October.

It was fortunate for René Bazin that delicate

health in childhood caused him to be brought up in the country, and to run wild in its woods and fields, there to drink deep of

> ". . . the silence and the calm
> Of mute insensate things."

His cradle-song, he tells us, was the story of the peasant epic of the Vendéen War. The events of his life were the episodes in the growth of plants and trees. These he relates in a delightful volume of recollections of childhood (published in 1897), called, after his old nurse, *Contes de Bonne Perrette*. Here he tells how he and his little brother got lost in the woods, and bridged over a stream by branches cut from a willow. When they reached home, the boys were severely reprimanded for having damaged the woods of a neighbouring proprietor, an imposing old lady, who was a friend of the family. Furnished with an explanatory note, they were sent to make their apologies. Trembling with fear, they stood before the dignified dame ; but their sorrow was turned to joy when they heard that all the retribution demanded was a promise to return frequently and make the stream bank near the mutilated willow their playground.

In a charming introduction to this volume of recollections the author writes to the children to whom the book is dedicated: "You are at a delicious age. I have passed through it before you. And I have enjoyed it more fully and freely than others, having had the good fortune to pass a great part of my early youth in the country. I did little at *De Viris Illustribus*, but I learnt what is unteachable—to see the infinite in things, and to listen to its life. Instead of my horizon being bounded by the walls of a class-room or a courtyard, it was limited only by woods, meadows, the sky changing every hour, and a little stream changing too in concert. My friends were the mist, the sunshine, the twilight, where fear haunts you in your shadow; the flowers, whose dynasties I knew better than those of the kings of Egypt; the birds whose names are written in the motion of their flight; the dwellers on the land, who are silent mysterious persons. I remember that on certain days my heart overflowed with gladness, and became so light that it seemed ready to soar away and melt into space. I was reaping my harvest without knowing it. Since then I have realised how lasting a treasure is the wealth of impressions garnered in those days."

The friends of Bazin's childhood, trees, meadows, woods, and streams, are to be met with over and over again in his novels. The story of one of them, the lime-tree under which his mother used to sew and embroider, is delightfully told in *Les Recits de la Plaine et de la Montagne*.

"I think," he writes, "it was the last of what was once a lime-tree alley. The tree was in the form of a fan, and God only knows how many flowers the summer strewed upon it. The bees hovered over it in swarms; its scent was wafted right on to the road; so that one day a poor woman came in with a basket and said to my mother, 'Madame, will you sell me some lime-blossom for my little girl, who sleeps badly?'

"To buy or to borrow, every one knows what that means. She went away with her basket full. 'There,' said my mother, pointing to the tree, 'you would never see the difference.' The next year the same woman came back, but with another basket, which was twice as big as the first. The tree gave her its flowers. My mother said to me: 'She has done well; there still remains on the tree quite as much as we want.' The third year, the woman, to whom custom had now given rights to the tree's produce, arrived pushing a little cart, in which was placed an empty cradle. All the flowers had to be gathered in order to fill this cradle. My mother was not there, and we allowed her to take them. When my mother came back and saw the pillage, she smiled still more sweetly than before, and said: 'This time, I am very glad; so many lime trees are quite useless!'"

This trivial incident, related with such a tender French grace and delicate charm, gives an excellent idea of the spirit of the writer's work. Here we see his loving tenderness overflowing alike towards inanimate nature and towards those taciturn, often inscrutable, beings who inhabit the country side.

Bazin has lived side by side with the country folk, and has learned to know their hearts. He treats them seriously. He is not contented to pass on his way with an amused smile at their vagaries, like a certain distinguished Parisian novelist who, when spending a few weeks in a country village, writes of the villagers as if they were entertaining children. This Parisian relates how he went into a village shop to ask for white notepaper, and was told that it was only kept in the jam-making season. And with a laughing superiority he reflects: "Happy people, they cannot imagine that notepaper can serve for anything but to cover jam-pots; thus live the peasants; they are happy and they are wise; true wisdom is to demand little from the earth and from destiny." So the Parisian philosopher passes on his way, in reality knowing nothing of the lives and thoughts of people who live outside towns. His true companions in the village are, as he tells us, the dogs, the geese, the hens, and a big horse called Bibi.

"To townspeople the country is nearly always silent," says Bazin.[1] Passers-by do not hear its voice. Even if you converse with the reaper, the woodcutter, or the man hoeing, you will not get to know him. He will reply to you in words embarrassed and intentionally trivial, and then he will be silent. Do not trust either to a few weeks' visit to some corner of France or Navarre. In order to conquer this cautious hero you must regu-

[1] *Questions Littéraires et Sociales les Personnages de Roman*, 1906.

larly lay siege to him. The silent creature will be appealed to alone by cordiality, by your inhabiting with him a country bounded by the same limited horizon, by your meeting him often at the turning of the ways, and above all by the slow persuasion that you, like him, love the land, from the clover and the grain not yet sprouted to the magpie's nest darkly adorning the crest of the oak."

Such are the methods by which Bazin has entered into close communion with the rustic, by which he has laid bare his heart and learnt how to make him a living personage in the novel. With the idle, fashionable life of towns Bazin is not concerned. His theme is work. Of the passion of love he has but little to say, and that little is but indifferently said. "Love," he writes, "is only an episode, a spectator, or sometimes a firework of life, and occasionally its guiding lamp. But whether or no that lamp be burning, work continues unremitting, the inflexible law of humanity." All Bazin's best characters belong to the labouring classes. "It is predicted that to-morrow these working men will be our masters," he writes, "and it is probable that we shall do their work as they are doing ours. It is important therefore that we should know each other. Many who have not seen them at home will be not unwilling to have them described before making their nearer acquaintance."

In 1904 Bazin was elected a member of the French Academy, which eight years previously had crowned his published works collectively. His reception was by the late Monsieur Ferdinand Brunetière, who, in an illuminating speech, according to the very highest traditions of that famous assembly, sketched the outline of the new Academician's literary career. Bazin's novels, said Monsieur Brunetière, fall into two distinct groups, separated by a period of travel in Sicily, Italy, and Spain which began in 1893. His early stories, *Stéphanette*, *Ma Tante Giron*, *Une Tache d'Encre*, *Les Noellet*, *A l'Aventure*, *La Sarcelle Bleue*, while distinguished by sweetness and charm, lack consistency, force, and colour. "There are not enough wolves in your sheep-cotes," said Brunetière, "and the few who do succeed in breaking through are speedily transformed into something like lambs." But travel in Sicily, Italy, and Spain worked a wondrous change in Bazin's genius. On his return he saw

France with new eyes. His hand applied itself more diligently to paint what he saw. His knowledge of humanity widened. His talent became more supple, and his personality grew stronger. Now he was able to reap the harvest of those impressions he had received during the happy years of his childhood.

Comparing the French peasants and workmen with their Latin cousins in other parts of Europe, he gained fresh insight into their character. Mysteries of their nature hitherto incomprehensible were now revealed. The countryside itself assumed a newer and more distinct aspect, and a stronger individuality when compared with foreign scenes. "Landscapes like us have relatives," writes Bazin. "I was surprised to find so much of Italy in the men and the neighbourhood of Lyons."

Bazin had now attained the complete development of his talent. Since 1893 he has produced four masterpieces descriptive of peasant life and country scenery in various parts of France: *La Terre qui Meurt*, *Les Oberlé*, *Donatienne*, and finally *Le Blé qui Lève*. In these books the author paints with incomparable skill the marshy plains of La Vendée, the bleak, barren heaths of Brittany, the majestic forests and rich pastures of the centre, and the wooded slopes and smiling valleys of the Vosges. His plots meanwhile have attained to a consistency of structure lacking in his earlier works. While neither of these books can be called a problem novel, the writer permits himself to touch on certain questions of the hour: the abandonment of the country for the town in *La Terre qui Meurt* and *Donatienne*, the Germanisation of Alsace and Lorraine in *Les Oberlé*, the tyranny of trades unions in *Le Blé qui Lève.* But the main theme throughout is the love of the peasant for his native soil. The heroes of these novels are true sons of mother earth, *vrais terriens* their creator calls them. Their language is such as peasants would naturally use: simple, direct, rough sometimes, but never affecting coarseness. "You have never confounded strength with violence nor more especially with grossness," says Brunetière. The delight of Bazin's peasants is to reflect "on simple and ancient matters, and in them contemplation is the sign of their vocation, the mark of the glorious condition of those who feed the world."

In *La Terre qui Meurt* it seems to André

Lumineau, returning from military service in Algeria, that he receives a glad welcome from the very soil of his native homestead. "There was not a clod of earth that did not greet him, not a reed in the ditch, not a trimmed elm that did not welcome him with a friendly glance."

André is the last remaining healthy son of old Père Lumineau, the farmer of La Fromentière. His eldest brother Mathurin is a cripple. His second brother François and his eldest sister Eléonore, bored by the loneliness of the country, and shrinking from hard unremunerative toil, have gone to live in the town. The old father Lumineau looks to André to revive the prosperity of La Fromentière. But André in his turn grows weary and despairs of rendering fruitful the exhausted land of the old farm. He hears of virgin soil in the Far West which with little labour brings forth abundantly. Yet he hesitates long before emigrating. He is a devoted son and he loves his youngest sister Roussille. "Moreover the *Vendéen*," says Bazin, "holds more strongly than any other French provincial to the soil on which he was born." And it is with many a misgiving that André finally decides to quit his native land. One of the strongest passages in the book is that describing André's departure, which nearly breaks his old father's heart. It was late in the February afternoon : the farmer, his daughter, and his farm servant were sitting in the barn, weaving willow wands into baskets.

"The rain came down more heavily and the air grew keener and colder. There was a veil of mist between the barn and the house. The workers were dimly lighted by a light, coming one knew not whither, uncertain of its way like the rain and apparently driven by the wind. The ducks in the marsh were cackling with delight; the sparrows were twittering on the rafters of the roof. Not a word passed between the farmer, his daughter, and the servant.

"Toussaint Lumineau was gazing at Roussille. He looked at her oftener and more attentively than usual. He was thinking: She is all that remains to me. The white willow remained motionless in his hand. The memory of his other children was coming over him in a gust like the rain. In his heart's most secret chamber, the father was crying: 'François? André?' He was trying to figure to himself that little place marked America on the map. Where in the wide world was his son now? In a town? On the road? On the sea which swallows up men? Toussaint Lumineau endeavoured to join him in spirit. But his effort was vain. All the roads of his mind lost themselves in the unknown.

"Far away, that very hour, a soul was beholding in all the clearness of a familiar picture —La Fromentière and its elms, the father, Roussille, Mathurin, the meadows of the marsh, and the surrounding Vendée.

"He was the child of whom the father spoke with the greatest regret, of whom were thinking, in all the poverty of their simple imaginations, the two basket-weavers and the servant who was splitting the willow wands. A stranger, unknown, worn out with having passed the night in the train, and the afternoon in hurrying to emigration agencies, he was seated on bales of sheepskins bound together with iron, in the docks of a great port, awaiting the hour of embarkation on the steamship that was to carry him away. Before him lay the Scheldt, rolling its waters in half circles, hurling them with a loud noise against the quay, a mighty river appearing from the mist on the left, disappearing into the mist on the right, everywhere of equal breadth, and everywhere covered with ships. André's tired gaze followed the forms crossing each other, sailing-boats, steamers, coasting and fishing vessels, all coloured grey by the mist and the declining day, mingling for a moment, then separating and gliding on their separate ways. But especially he looked beyond at the low ground surrounded by a bend in the river, at the meadows saturated with moisture, deserted, infinite, seeming to float on the pale waters. How they reminded him of the country he had forsaken! How they spoke to his heart! Nothing distracted him, not the rolling of the trucks, nor the captains' whistles, nor the voices of thousands of men of all nations coming off the vessels around him, and moving under the sheds of corrugated iron. Neither was he interested in the great town stretching behind him, whence there floated now and then over the noises of labour the sound of a peal of bells, such as he had never heard before.

"Meanwhile the hour was approaching. He felt his emotion increasing. The noise of a troop of people walking made him turn round. They were emigrants coming out of the sheds where the agents had penned them, and, crossing the quay, in one long column, grey as the mist.

" Long did André Lumineau look before joining them. He was seeking a French face. Finding none, he took his place in the rank. . . . He was wearing his cavalry cloak, of which only the buttons had been altered. His neighbours glanced at him indifferently, and accepted him without a word. With them he crossed the hundred metres that separated him from the boat, walked up the incline, and gained the gangway, which was already being raised by the swell of the river. Then while the others, those who had relations or friends in the crowd, walked in groups past the machinery or descended the ladders, he, in the stern of the ship, leant over the side to try if he could still see the river and its grey meadows, for a host of memories rushed in upon him, and his courage was failing.

" Near him, leaning over the barrier, there was an old woman, still fresh-featured, wrapped in a black cloak with a cape, whose cap was fixed by two gold-headed pins. She was rocking a child in her arms. André did not look at her. But she, who, in the turmoil and confusion of the boat's starting, could not rest her eyes anywhere, sometimes raised them towards the foreigner standing near her, who must be thinking of home. Perhaps she had a son of the same age. Pity took possession of her; and, although she was quite sure her neighbour would not understand her language, the old woman said:

"'*O heeft pyn?*'

"When she had repeated it several times, he understood from the word *pyn*, and the accent she put on it, that the woman asked him whether he were in trouble. He replied:

"'Yes, madame.'

"The old mother stroked André's hand with her own, damp and cold with the mist, and the young Vendean wept, for he remembered his own mother's caresses just like those, and she also on feast days wore a white cap and gilt ornaments.

"Over the Vendean marsh the same mist was driving as had passed over the plains of Scheldt. From time to time, as Roussille held out to him the trembling willow twigs, Toussaint Lumineau looked at them as if they had been the masts of tossing vessels. Now and again he gazed meditatively at his last child, and Roussille felt that it gave him pleasure to look at her. A squall broke over the elms, tore them and beat their branches on the roof of La Fromentière. The crevices of the barn, the gutters, the tiles, the ends of the rafters, the angles of the walls, whistled all together. And the sound, sharp and agonising, went out across the marsh.

"Three hundred leagues away a siren's shriek rent the air. The prow of a great steamer drove the water before it and advanced slowly, still half inert and drifting. The emigrants, outcasts from the old world, nameless sufferers, grew frightened as the earth failed from beneath them. Thoughts travelled along different roads to the old homes. The handsome André Lumineau passed away into the darkness.

"The farmer threw back a handful of willows into the tub. 'Let us go in,' he said; 'we can see to work no longer.'"

Bazin's sympathetic painting of the country and her peasants recalls Loti's similar treatment of the sea and her sailors. The earth is as much a personage for Bazin as the sea is for Loti. In *La Terre qui Meurt* the peasants of the coast are imbued with that same poetic melancholy which is one of the greatest charms of Loti's Breton seamen. Bazin's peasants and Loti's fishermen are alike haunted by vague dreams when the sea-wind blows over the dunes. They are alike imbued with the fundamental melancholy of the peasants of the coast. Nowhere is this poetic melancholy more intense than in *Donatienne*, a novel, which appeared in 1902. On this powerful story Monsieur Brunetière bestowed high praise. "I do not think," he said, "that the instinctive, unconscious yet divine philosophy of repentance and pardon has ever been better expressed, or in terms simpler and stronger in any tale by Dickens or Maupassant."

The story is of a poor Breton cotter, Jean Louarne, and his wife, Donatienne. In the opening chapter poverty is casting a gloom over the humble dwelling. The Louarnes are finding the little plot of barren earth on which they depend for a living insufficient to support them and their three children—Noémi, a little girl of five, her younger sister Lucienne, and the baby Joel, an infant at the breast. Like many of her Breton sisters, Donatienne, in order to save her family from ruin, abandons her own baby and goes to Paris to be foster-mother to the child of rich parents. Fond mother as she is, and morally superior to her fellow-servants through her country breeding, the temptations of the capital are too much for her. "She was pretty, *la petite Bretonne*, with her white coif and her nurse's long ribbons. People turned round to look at her as she passed. The men admired her. She was so young, so light-hearted, so vain, so fond of pleasure. In six months the work of perdition was well advanced." Her home letters grow fewer and fewer, then cease altogether. She begins to be ashamed of being married to a rustic. Her husband's appeals for money are disregarded, his announcements of impending disaster disbelieved. The little Breton homestead is sold. Louarne, with his two children and the baby in a little cart, tramp in search of work into La Vendée.

Bazin's insight into peasant character is forcibly revealed in the story of Louarne's pilgrimage.

"He travelled for two or three days, then stopped at some farm to work for his bread. Here or there the groan of the threshing-machine was always to be heard in the morning; and it was enough for him to present himself and to say, 'Will you engage me?' to be accepted among the bands of men and women, as numerous as the guests at a wedding, who surrounded the machine and served it. Everywhere, in spite of the fatigue of the farmers' wives, who had to prepare dinner for so many, the children were taken in, and some one was found more or less quickly, more or less willingly, to boil the baby's broth and wash his clothes. The men, when they saw the little cart, nearly always said 'No.' The women said 'Yes,' and let it come in and stay. But when Louarne left the farm, they never failed to warn him and to predict, pointing to Joel, 'You will kill him, my poor man! When the bad weather comes you will see what will happen! One does not tramp through France with an infant child.'"

Their predictions came true, and in the bad weather poor little Joel fell ill. But the solidarity of the poor declared itself; a woman working in the field had compassion on the child. "She took him in her arms, raised him to her breast and said: 'I take him for myself.' It was adoption."

In the end Louarne, joined on the road by a rough woman who takes his lost wife's place, finds regular work in a Vendean quarry.

Years pass. Sorrow, labour, exposure to the air, mistrust of himself and his fellow-men had made of the Breton emigrant a very statue of poverty. His eyes roved restlessly over that country of calm hills unassailed by the tempest. "They found no place whereon to rest: neither on the crops, which in no way resembled those of the country of Ploeuc, his native village, nor on the ponds, which, glistening here and there on the tableland, made him think of the sea, nor on the houses of the neighbouring village. Many years' habitation of the place had not made him feel at home in it. Louarne remained as on his arrival, a travelling day labourer who is tolerated, a foreigner who is mistrusted."

A terrible catastrophe breaks the monotony of his dull existence. A fall of rock from the quarry renders Louarne a cripple. In their misfortune he and his children are abandoned by the woman, who had only attached herself to him because his plight had seemed a little less miserable than her own. Now, when the condition of the Louarne family seems utterly hopeless, a ray of light comes from an unexpected quarter. Donatienne in Paris, who, as far as her husband was concerned, seems to have possessed no heart at all, has never forgotten her children. She had found it hard to part from them; she had often murmured over their names in her heart—Noémi, Lucienne, Joel, the last especially, whom she was nursing when she left, and of whom her foster-child in Paris had reminded her. By chance she meets a Vendean who puts her in communication with her eldest daughter, Noémi, now a girl in her teens, and Donatienne returns to her family. She relinquishes a life of comparative ease and indulgence to return to the paths of duty. As she looks at her worn, crippled husband, "she who had sinned and suffered had pity." With peasant simplicity and common sense she takes up the task abandoned by the other woman.

"It is time to get supper," she said to Noémi. "Give me the sabots of her who has gone. I will go and draw the water and prepare the soup for you all."

Such is the conclusion of *Donatienne*. Those who read the whole book will agree that it is indeed a masterpiece. Like the *Iliad* or some Greek frieze, it does not finish, it breaks off. There are times to knit up all and make an end, but there are also times for these Homeric methods.

Le Blé qui Lève, Bazin's last novel, is filled

with the same pious love of nature as *Donatienne.* Here, in place of the undulating plains of Brittany and La Vendée, we have the tall rocks, the mountains, and the deep and gloomy woods of central France. "Here the conservatism of the country," writes Bazin, "is being invaded by the worst political passions; words are being used that have not been heard for centuries." In an earlier and greatly inferior novel, *De toute son Âme*, he had touched on the great duel between capital and labour in the towns. Now in *Le Blé qui Lève* we see the tyranny of trades unionism in the country, among the woodcutters in the forests of La Nièvre. The members of the gang are powerfully described. It includes some striking types: the worthless Lureux, who, when the Count addressed him, took care to be rude, not from any personal hatred, but for fear his comrades should accuse him of talking to a *bourgeois;* Ravoux, the President of the Union, a pale man with a black beard, a theorist, a dreamer, who remained coldly silent when his comrades sang "L'Internationale." The most human, the most sympathetic of the woodcutters is Gilbert Cloquet, An intelligent, laborious workman, he is a true native of La Nièvre, "where the will is strong, even violent, but where the face is cold and the tongue often silent." Once he had been handsome; but fifty years of poverty had withered his face, had gathered shadows round his bright eyes, and caused the veins on his temple to stand out, but his profile still bore traces of refinement, and his beard, still fair, fringed his chin nobly and gave to Gilbert Cloquet the air of a northener, a Scandinavian or a Norman descended among the pastures and the forests of the centre.

Gilbert had formerly been the leader of his comrades and the President of the Union; but his moderation had rendered him unpopular, and he is suspected of being a traitor to the cause. When, without consulting his fellow-workmen, he agrees to cut down the trees of a copse belonging to Count Michel, the other woodcutters accuse him of violating the rules of the Union, and attack him at his work. As he lies in bed recovering from the wounds inflicted by his comrades, the President Ravoux brings him hush-money; but Gilbert assures him he had never intended to prosecute his assailants.

In striking contrast to these woodcutters,

all of whom, with the exception of Gilbert, are filled with bitter class hatred, stand out the liberal and enlightened landed proprietors, the Count Michel de Maximieu and Monsieur Jacquemin. By replanting the forests, restocking the farms, and introducing new methods of agriculture, these landholders desire to serve the soil, and through the soil to serve France.

In the opening paragraphs of the story, the Count, instructed by his spendthrift father to raise money by selling timber on the estate, is hesitating as to the fate of an ancient oak tree; he cannot bear to have it felled; and in the end he decides that the money must be obtained in some other way. The scene recalls Madame de Sèvigné's dirge over the trees on her Breton estate, cut down to provide for the extravagance of her prodigal son. Wondering whether some one of these venerable oaks, like that wherein Clorinda dwelt, had not once uttered speech, weeping over the desolate dryads driven from their dwelling in these horrid woods (*dans l'horreur de ces bois*), she turns disconsolate from her vanishing groves, and not even the excellent supper, prepared for her by Le Premier *Président* and his wife, is able to raise her spirits.

We have travelled far since a passage like this was thought to reveal an appreciation of natural scenery. In the interval Rousseau has brought the note of green into literature. And Monsieur de Maximieu's oaks have no need to borrow a fantastic life from Dryads and Clorindas, for they are living creatures in themselves, having a personality all their own.

The charm of the forest in *Le Blé qui Lève*, recalling scenes in Hardy's *Woodlanders*, lives with an equal grace in Bazin's earlier novel, *Les Oberlé*. Here amid the dark pine-trees of the Vosges, and the simple lives of the peasants in the valleys, Bazin lays the scene of one of those tragedies of racial antagonism, of that duel between the two rival civilisations of the French eastern borderland.

The Oberlé family is divided against itself. The father and daughter are allowing themselves to be germanised; the mother and son, true to France, are hostile to everything German. In the end the son deserts from the German army, and crosses the frontier into France to serve in the army of the country he loved although he had never seen. The characters of this novel, through a certain paleness of colouring, lack distinctness and fail to interest. The love scenes between the son Jean Oberlé and Odile Bastian, and between the sister Lucienne Oberlé and the German officer to whom she is betrothed, are, like other love scenes in Bazin's novels, singularly stiff and constrained.

In strong contrast to the comparative woodenness of these love passages is the natural simplicity of the descriptions of country life: the Easter pilgrimage to the summit of St. Odile, that sacred mountain of Alsace, so beautifully described by Barrès in *Au Service de l'Allemagne:* the hop-picking at Monsieur Bastian's in the hop-yard high up on the mountain slope, near the borders of the woodland.

The gathering of the hops is a great event in this Alsatian village. Early in the day all the women may be seen wending their ways to the hop-garden as to a festival. The actual hop-picking takes place in the afternoon in the farmyard in the valley, to which are carried in carts the strands of hops cut down in the morning. "There the women and girls, seated on chairs and stools in two long lines, an avenue of fair heads swaying among the leaves, which, stretching from one woman to another, unite them like a garland, each with a basket on her right and on her left a heap of hops, pick off the flowers and throw away the bare stems."

In such clearly drawn pictures of country life resides the excellence of *Les Oberlé*. The cases of conscience with which the novel fairly bristles are too numerous. The book borders on the problem novel. *L'Isolée*, a book published in 1905, belongs entirely to this *genre*. It is a novel with a purpose, and far from being one of the author's best works, ranks considerably below *La Terre qui Meurt* and *Donatienne*.

Its occasion was the law against religious associations. What he considers to be the disastrous consequences of this measure, Bazin attempts to demonstrate by the history of Sister Pascale, *l'Isolée*. But no impartial reader will think that the author makes out a good case for the congregations.

The pretty Sister Pascale, like a mediæval anchorite, is intent on saving her own precious soul. Although an only child, she determines to forsake her old father, lately bereaved of his wife, and to become a nun. With sad resignation her father asks: "Is it to tend the sick in our Lyons hospitals that you are leaving me?"

"No, papa; I am going to join the sisters of Saint Hildegarde."

"And to teach children?"

"To work out my own salvation," a low voice replied.

It was consciousness of her own weakness and desire for a strict rule of life that led Pascale to become a nun. She found counsel and support in the little community of the five sisters of Saint Hildegarde. She rejoiced to know that holy souls were guarding and defending her from those powers of evil she so much dreaded. It seemed just possible, so we are told, that, watched over by four holy women, this weak sister might develop into a saint. Then came the dissolution of the community. When this group of five was scattered and Pascale could no longer be propped up by the four holy women, she moved in worlds not realised and fainted by the way. "What will become of me without you all?" she had asked. "The peace of my soul when I entered Saint Hildegarde was the thought that it was for ever. And now! and now!" Pascale goes to Nîmes to a cousin, Madame

Prayou, and her handsome and attractive son Jules; he is in reality a clever blackguard, and a bully of the very worst type. Of course it was inevitable that a weak, simple, pretty girl like Pascale should fall a victim to the deep-laid schemes of such a man. In a short time she becomes his chattel, and is reduced to the lowest depth of degradation. Her former Mother Superior comes to rescue her, and is on the point of carrying her away from her persecutor when he drags her back. A second attempt at rescue ends in the murder of Pascale by her lover.

This sensational conclusion is unworthy of the author's genius and of that artistic skill revealed in *La Terre qui Meurt* and *Donatienne*. *L'Isolée* has an air of being written to order. Were there a Religious Tract Society in Catholic France this novel might well be included among its publications. The characters of the book are overdrawn; the situations are forced: the perfect holiness and unity of the sisters of Saint Hildegarde are not for this world; the outrageous villainy of Jules Prayou is improbable in one who at first sight appeared a gentleman. The conclusion of the novel is weak. According to *L'Isolée*, the chief object of religious sisterhoods is to provide a refuge from life's temptations and a nursery of holiness for such weak creatures as Pascale. It were better to provide an asylum for the feeble-minded and to call it by that name.

Nevertheless there are redeeming features in the book. Two characters strongly drawn are those of the temporising priest, Canon le Suet, the typical trimmer, and his self-sacrificing, ascetic brother, l'Abbé Monéchal. When asked for counsel Le Suet replied with words that might be read in any newspaper. "The times are hard, but with good will on both sides everything will be arranged. Even Catholics have made mistakes. Certainly you have reason to complain, and I am sorry for you; but you should have foreseen what would happen, and done this or that before it was too late." Canon le Suet cries, "Peace, peace," when there is no peace. For him peace comes before everything, even before the honour of the religion in which he believes. When the sisters of Saint Hildegarde, menaced with expulsion, seek his advice, they are told to submit; the abbé reminds them that he had prophesied all these things, and regrets that his warning was vain. "Sacrifice yourselves . . . let the whirlwind pass," is his counsel. Very different is the advice given by the Abbé Monéchal to the perplexed sisters. He is a hard-working priest who has devoted his life to the service of others. When the sisters enter his humble study they find him exhausted by the day's labours, fallen asleep with his head on the plain deal table. He awakes, and they tell him of the threatening misfortune. "You have not the strength to resist. . . . But you must not go away willingly," he tells them. "You must yield only to force. It is not necessary for there to be any noise and dealing of blows, but it is necessary that there should be witnesses to say one day, 'They did not willingly leave us; they were driven out; they would like to return: let us recall them.'"

Bazin relates the facts of the sisters' expulsion with a moderation admirable in a Catholic writer, and with a cleverness and restraint which impel conviction. The eviction scene throws an interesting light on the crisis through which the French Church has been passing:—

"Almost immediately a ring was heard at the front door. Sister Justine turned pale and said, 'Come.' She rose rapidly, went down the passage, and, drawing herself up, with a firm gesture opened the door of her school and her house.

"Two men saluted her, one by raising his felt hat, bowing slightly with an obvious desire to be correct, the other by an expression of his mean and bilious countenance. It was the commissioner of police and his clerk.

"Sister Justine drew back two steps. 'You permit me to come in?' asked the big man, buttoned tight in his frockcoat. And without waiting, he advanced sideways, his right shoulder first by reason of his huge breadth. He did not wish to explain himself on the doorstep and to cause passers-by to gather round the groups already formed in the square. His clerk slipped in behind him and almost completely closed the door.

"'You are in the house of two of my sisters of Clermont-Ferrand,' said the Superior. 'You come to take possession of their goods.'

"'I have already told you that is no concern of mine.'

"'I protest in their name, sir.'

"'Please do it briefly,' said this pseudo *bourgeois*, who had performed this function before.

"Sister Justine signed to him to be silent.

"'Oh!' she said, 'you need not fear; I will not make you a speech. But I tell you, in order that you may repeat it, that you commit three acts of injustice: you are about to destroy my school for poor Christian children, to seize our goods, and to drive us from our home. Now expel me.'

"The police officer made a wry face. 'I would rather you did not oblige me to resort to any show of force.'

"'I insist upon it. I yield to nothing else.'

"'As you wish.'

"Sister Justine turned round.

"'Are you there, sisters?' . . .

"Sister Justine looked at the police officer.

"'Perform your office.'

"The man with some timidity put his hand on the black veil which covered Sister Justine's shoulder and arm, and, following the superior, preceded by the commissioner, the four sisters appeared on the threshold and descended the steps."

Such is a Catholic's account of one of those scenes of eviction which two years ago were common throughout France. Its dignified strain justifies Brunetière's criticism when he congratulated Bazin on never "raising his voice," not even when he dealt with the gravest questions of the hour.

These sisters of Saint Hildegarde, like Bazin's French peasants, possess the same pathetic charm as Millet's field-workers and Wordsworth's leech-gatherer. Bazin is no pessimist like our own great peasant novelist, Hardy. Bazin's Christian faith teaches him that in the end good will triumph over evil. At present it is true the hearts of men are bad; the ideal of fraternity seems far from being realised. But Bazin sees the evil in the world held in check by an army of consolers, through whom society is enabled to bear its suffering. "They understand sorrow even before they have suffered. They divine it wherever it is; while incapable of destroying it, they command it silently, control it, hold it by their charm, like a beast whose ferocity ceases to be harmful as long as they are by."

EDOUARD ROD

THE WORKS OF EDOUARD ROD

1879. Le Développement de la Légende d'Œdipe dans l'Histoire de la Littérature.
A propos de l'Assommoir.
1880. Les Allemands à Paris.
1881. **Palmyre Veulard.**
1882. Côte à Côte.
La Chute de Miss Topsy.
1884. **L'Autopsie du Docteur Z. et autres Nouvelles.**
La Femme d'Henri Vanneau.
1885. **La Course à la Mort.**
1886. De la Littérature comparée.
Tatiana Deïlof.
1887. Les Malavoglia.
1888. Etudes sur le XIX. Siècle.
Le Sens de la Vie.
1890. **Les Trois Cœurs.**
Scènes de la vie Cosmopolite.
1891. Stendhal.
Dante.
1891. **Nouvelles Romandes.**
Les Idées Morales du Temps Présent.
1892. **La Sacrifiée.**
1893. Lamartine.
La Vie Privée de Michel Teissier.
1894. Michel Teissier. (Drama.)
La Seconde Vie de Michel Teissier.
Le Silence.
1895. **Les Roches Blanches.**
1896. Scènes de la Vie Suisse.
Dernier Refuge.
1897. **L 'Innocente.**
Là Haut.
1898. Essai sur Goethe.
Le Ménage du Pasteur Naudié.
1899. Nouvelles Etudes sur le XIX. Siècle.
Morceaux Choisis des Littératures Etrangères.
1900. **Au Milieu du Chemin.**
1901. **Mademoiselle Annette.**
1902. **L'Eau Courante.**
1903. **L'Inutile Effort.**
Nouvelles Vaudoises.
1905. **Un Vainqueur.**
L'Indocile.
1906. L'Affaire Jean Jacques Rousseau.
Le Réformateur. (Drama.)
Reflets d'Amérique.
1907. **L'Ombre s'etend sur la Montagne.**

EDOUARD ROD, 1857

"I have always thought that the most truly tragic subject is the moral problem."—FERDINAND BRUNETIÈRE.

THE political, social, and religious controversies which have rent France in twain during the last ten years have profoundly affected the world of letters. Many of these disputes have been led by literary men; and even novelists have come down from the mount of pure contemplation into the arena of warfare. Emile Zola set the example. He was followed by Anatole France, Paul Bourget, Marcel Prévost, and many others. Thus the French public has come to expect its novelists to espouse definitely one side or the other in questions of the day.

Monsieur Rod is one of the few French novelists who refuse to be identified with any particular party, and his aloofness gives rise to a multitude of conjectures as to his future intellectual destiny. Some months ago, when he went to Rome and wrote thence to the *Figaro*, an eloquent letter on the historical greatness of the Roman Church, there was a loud outcry that at last he had shown his hand, that at length there was no longer any doubt as to his religious opinions, that he was about to follow the example of Huysmans and Bourget and to join the Church of Rome.

But Monsieur Rod has not yet forsaken the world and entered a Benedictine monastery, nor has he openly espoused the cause of clericalism. The effect of these conjectures on the mind of Monsieur Rod himself may be inferred from a paragraph in his last novel, *L'Ombre s'étend sur la Montagne*, where he writes of the philosophical author, Monsieur Jaffé: "He was discussed with that violence always provoked by sincere writing in times of public agitation. Freethinkers considered him an apostate because he broke with their traditions and emancipated himself from their tyranny; conservatives hailed him as an unexpected recruit because he approved of certain items in their programme; one newspaper announced his imminent conversion; another maintained that he had gone to Rome to receive the papal benediction. He read all this without anger or astonishment, somewhat moved, however, to see what self-interest, discord, civil hatred, intolerance, and fanaticism will discover in the simple work of a detached investigator (*un chercheur désinteressé*)."

In this last expression, Monsieur Rod describes himself exactly; for he is above all things *un chercheur désinteressé*, a detached patient investigator of human life,

> "holding no form of creed,
> But contemplating all."

His inquiries have led him through many phases of experience, ranging from what he now holds to have been anarchic individualism to the serener air of collectivism. But throughout his spirit moves in a pessimistic cloud; he never escapes entirely from that moulding force of his early genius, the influence of Schopenhauer.

His novels are one long indictment of human life; and in his latest production, as well as in his first important work, he often appears to regard death as the one good thing in existence. But such an attitude is something of a pose. Occasionally he comes to himself and is sincere; then he confesses that life, terrible, cruel, iniquitous though it be, is better than annihilation.

Some of this pessimism may be the result of heredity and early environment. Though by choice and avocation he is a Parisian and an agnostic—" Paris is the city of my choice; I believe in her and love her"—*Paris demeure ma ville d'election, j'ai foi en Paris et je l'aime,*[1] he writes—by birth he is a Swiss and a Calvinist. Both the manner and the matter of his novels betray his origin. They are full of the romantic poetry of the Swiss, while they lack the ethereal grace of style, the concise crispness of phrase which reveal the true Frenchman. The working out of their plots is too often in accord with that fatalism which, resulting from the Calvinistic creed of his boyhood, caused him to choose as the theme of his university thesis the *Development of the Legend of Œdipus.*

Hereditary influences were not alone in casting a gloom over the author's youthful spirit. What should have been the gladsome years of childhood, were passed by the sick couch of his paralysed mother. " A sad event completed my development," he writes in one of his novels. " My mother was stricken with

[1] *La Course à la Mort.*

paralysis; I became her nurse; she was dying slowly while I was growing up."[1]

The picture of human suffering thus engraved upon his memory has profoundly influenced his whole work. If there be one message more than another he considers it to be his duty to deliver it is that contained in his earliest great work:[2] "*Prostrate yourselves before the suffering of humanity.*"

Edouard Rod was born in 1857 at Nyon, a picturesque town, figuring in more than one of his novels, on the Lake of Geneva. His grandfather had been a schoolmaster; and his father in early manhood had followed the same calling, and then relinquished it for that of a bookseller. Many months of the boy Edouard's childhood were passed with his invalid mother in peasants' cottages in villages whither she had gone in search of health. In these humble abodes her son learnt to love that simple life which he was later to reproduce with graphic touch in such novels as *L'Eau Courante* and *Là Haut.*

When he was at home he attended first that dame school described in one of the most delightful of his idyllic novels, *Mademoiselle*

[1] *Au Milieu du Chemin.* [2] *La Course à la Mort.*

Annette, and later the college of Nyon. At fifteen he entered the Academy of Lausanne, and attended the lectures of the philosopher, Charles Secretan, whose originality and breadth of thought was one of the moulding influences of his boyhood. From Lausanne he passed to the University of Bonn, and from Bonn to Berlin, where he developed a passion for Wagner's music.

He was now studying his doctor's thesis, the completion of which took him to Paris, where he arrived in 1878, just after the appearance of Zola's *L'Assommoir*, when the controversy it excited was at its height. Into this controversy the young writer boldly plunged, and made his début in letters by a powerful pamphlet entitled *A Propos de l'Assommoir*, in which he defended the Realists, and gave an excellent exposition of Zola's literary system. Having identified himself with the realistic school, and come under the personal influence of Zola, he produced four novels of his own on realistic lines: *Palmyre Veulard*, *Côte à Côte*, *La Chute de Miss Topsy*, *L'Autopsie du Docteur Z.*, and *La Femme d Henri Vanneau.*

These four volumes are greatly inferior to Monsieur Rod's later work. Although the writer has long since ceased to call himself a realist, he is still regarded as tarred with Zola's brush by the peasants of his native canton. When you ask these good people about their illustrious fellow-countryman, they shake their heads mournfully and murmur the terrible name of Zola, which to them means all that is impious and impure in a decadent age. These simple Vaudois, alas! will never read the later works of their compatriot. There they would find him painting with a loving and a reverent hand the wholesome life of his native town, and the health-giving toil of the Swiss peasants on the shores of their beautiful lake, under the shadow of their majestic mountains.

Monsieur Rod's realistic novels were merely a necessary phase through which his genius had to pass. It was obvious that they were the exercises of his 'prentice hand, and that he had not yet discovered his vocation. In 1885, he put realism on one side, and produced an entirely original work, *La Course à la Mort*.

Some years later, in his preface to *Trois Cœurs*, Monsieur Rod described his literary evolution from naturalism into something its exact contrary, something he is pleased to term *Intuitivisme*.

"Ten years ago," he writes, "at the beginning of my literary career, I was a realist, like all the young men of the day; for Zola had intoxicated us. . . .

"We dreamed of forming a school, a school which should have battles and victories, a first night, like that of *Hernani*, a general and captains, a Victor Hugo, a Sainte Beuve. . . .

"Alas! that dream was never realised, and for more than one reason. . . . In conviction we might be realists, in temperament we never were. . . . We had aspirations that could never be satisfied by realism, which was essentially self-satisfied, narrow, materialist, more curious about manners than character, about things than souls: we were, and we were becoming more and more, restless, idealist, in love with the infinite, caring little for manners, in things seeking always man."

Among the influences carrying further and further from realism the youth of the early eighties, says Rod, were Wagner's music, Schopenhauer's and Leopardi's pessimism, pre-Raphaelite painting, English poetry, and Russian novels. These influences were driven home to the minds of French youth by De Voguë's *Studies in Russian Novelists*, and

Bourget's *Essays on Contemporary Psychology*; and they resulted in the case of Rod in a determination to write a novel devoid of all concrete incident, the action of which should take place entirely in the heart.

This resolve took shape in his first novel of mark, *La Course à la Mort*, his favourite among his books, he tells us, and the one which has cost him the greatest effort. Here he strikes the keynote of his genius. The whole of his later work has been evolved from the tendencies displayed in this little book of two hundred and ninety-eight pages.

The extreme pessimism of this volume, a kind of catechism based on the philosophy of Schopenhauer, aroused a great outcry. Monsieur Rod was accused of corrupting the youth of France. So, in a preface to a later edition, he found it necessary to defend his position. This he did somewhat feebly by maintaining the erroneous distinction between man's intellectual and his practical life. Still later in *Au Milieu du Chemin* he disproved this very statement.

Somewhat mistaken and unwholesome as may be the teaching of *La Course à la Mort*, it is, nevertheless, a work of power and insight;

and it is indispensable reading for those who would understand the development of the writer's talent. Here we have the origin of the threefold cord of his subsequent work: his novels of pure passion, those of peasant life, and those dealing with social questions. In the two books which followed *La Course à la Mort*, *Le Sens de la Vie* and *Les Trois Cœurs*, Monsieur Rod continues in a series of more or less autobiographical studies the probing of his hero's heart, the analysis of a temperament which he himself has compared to that of René, Werther, and Lara. Of the most significant of these three novels, *Le Sens de la Vie*, Jules Lemaitre in *Les Contemporains* makes a striking analysis. For Rod the conclusion of the whole matter is that life has a meaning for those alone who believe and who love. He uses the word "believe" in the widest sense of the term.

These abstract studies in morals were followed by novels of pure passion. The first, *La Sacrifiée*, appeared in 1892; and then came *La Vie Privée de Michel Teissier* in 1893. Now the writer's fame crossed the Channel; and this novel, the plot of which, as the author hints, may have been suggested by Parnell's story, was translated into English. Its sequel, *La Seconde Vie de Michel Teissier*, in 1894, was followed in the next four years by *Le Silence*, *Les Roches Blanches*, *Le Dernier Refuge*, and *Le Ménage du Pasteur Naudié*. In this last we have a fine picture of life in a circle rarely depicted by French novelists, that of the Eglise Reformée of France, at La Rochelle and the University town of Montauban.

In all these books Monsieur Rod, with a masterly hand, treats of love beating against the barriers of social law and other human relations, ending in the death of passion or in the shipwreck of the individual. In his later works, notably *Au Milieu du Chemin*, and *L'Ombre s'etend sur la Montagne*, the same problem finds a different solution, the storm of passion is stilled in a compromise between love and law.

Monsieur Rod depicts passion with a power displayed by no other living writer. In such works as these we are reminded of the preponderant part love plays in French fiction, and love of the irregular sort. Why this is so was explained by Monsieur Rod, when, in 1898, at the invitation of his English readers, he came to London and lectured on the contemporary French novel at Stafford House. Then with intense seriousness and admirable lucidity of thought and expression, addressing an audience largely composed of writers and critics, he justified the French novelist's method of concentrating his attention on love. "The moment of love," said the lecturer, "is the decisive moment, the only moment indeed when one of those obscure beings, who would otherwise leave no trace in history, may become a hero—at least in the poetical sense—may develop his innate energy and show his soul in all its truth. And because in irregular love the soul conflict is most violent, because regular love, unopposed as it is by the barriers of law, duty, or faith, has no history, it is in irregular love that the French novelist finds his most significant subject."

From these novels of passion, Monsieur Rod to a great extent and of set purpose banishes descriptive passages in order to concentrate his attention on the movements of the soul. "Description," he writes, "appears to me fastidious, and above all things illusionary: it holds an important place, and yet says little and explains nothing."

When he does describe the natural surroundings of his characters it is nearly always because they illustrate their state of mind. In 1897, however, he published the first of a series of novels in which, contrary to his previous method, description of natural scenery counts for much. *Là Haut* was the earliest of those novels, the first of those prose idylls of the Alps and the Jura, in which Monsieur Rod appears as the Thomas Hardy of Switzerland. Even in *La Course à la Mort* his feverish soul had found relief in turning away from books *ces porte-voix où l'humanité a crié tous ses désirs a chanté tous ses rêves, a pleuré toutes ses douleurs.* Treading in the footsteps of Rousseau, he had gone back to the country of his boyhood, to "the virgin mountain air, to the healing sights of nature." "Can I do better than passively to contemplate its useless blooming? (*ses inutiles floraisons*)," he had asked in the despairing mood of *La Course à la Mort.*

Thus he came to write a series of novels in which the atmosphere is healthier and the life simpler than in *La Vie de Michel Teissier* and similar works. The disappointed worldling, Sterny, in *Là Haut*, the hardened millionaire, Pierre Denys Nicollet, in *Mademoiselle Annette*, alike find peace and healing on the high mountain tops in the contemplation "of the ample spaces of the sky," sharing the simple life of the Vaudois peasants. These novels are full of idyllic pictures of peasant life and Alpine landscapes. So strong is the writer's love of the mountain country that he returns almost to pagan nature worship; he actually personifies the mountains and the valleys. In *Là Haut*, the fatal fall of the Alpinist, whose love of the mountains had been the passion of his existence, seems, like that of Empedocles from Etna, to be the perfecting of a life-long communion with nature. The chief personage of this novel is the Alpine village of Vallanches, endowed with a life really more intense than that of its human inhabitants. The towering peak, La Tour aux Fées, seemed to live with a life active, personal, almost human," as it looked down on the painful evolution of the primitive pastoral hamlet into a bustling fashionable village, with a railway line and big hotels. The tragedy of this book lies in the strife between "those eternal enemies: those who would have the world remain motionless, and those who would change everything." It is obvious that Monsieur Rod is on the side of the former. Volland, the advocate of elementary simplicity, says to Monsieur Rarogne, the capitalist, "You say that money is a seed like any other. Yes, unfortunately. A sad seed, Monsieur de Rarogne, a seed which germinates in evil appetites, an accursed seed, which no ill wind had as yet wafted into this neighbourhood." Monsieur Rod is no believer in the religion of the millionaire. In his opinion it is neither money nor worldly prosperity that is the cause of happiness. Those who can content themselves with little are richer than those who are always longing for more.

Such is the suggestive doctrine underlying the most delightful of these prose idylls: *Mademoiselle Annette.* "This is a true story, a catastrophe of real life," writes the author in his first chapter, "barely understood as it unrolled itself before my eyes in childhood, the details of which, however, have remained engraved on my memory."

Mademoiselle Annette, with large brown eyes, dimpled chin, heavy coils of dark brown hair, is the writer's favourite heroine. She attains as near as possible to perfection. Indeed, it is hard to find a single fault in the character of this Swiss schoolmistress. Some of the author's happiest years were passed at her school, he tells us. "There he was too happy to need even friends." "Mademoiselle Annette Nicollet's school was one of those true schools of Thelema, which existed before pedagogy became a science; at a time when there was no question of overwork, when the alphabet was still a pretty picture-book, when every year did not bring the invention of some new method of making straight strokes, when recreation was much and lessons little."

But ruin came upon Mademoiselle Annette's family. She had her own disappointment of the heart. And then she found her joy in ministering to others, not with a martyr's air, but as one simply following the bent of her own inclination. In the end she softens the heart of her millionaire uncle, and converts him from the worship of his banking account to the belief that "the spirit of sacrifice is the greatest of virtues, that it alone can bring true contentment, that it can cause greater happiness than any other disposition of the soul."

The background of this simple story is the little town of Bielle, in reality Nyon, the author's birthplace, on the Lake of Geneva. Already in *La Course à la Mort* he had introduced his readers to the tranquillity of its grass-grown streets, to the sad majesty of its huge Protestant temple, whither his mother took him every Sunday, and outside which there stood an ancient statue, thought by some to represent a goddess and by others a Roman empress. The old-world life of this little town and its inhabitants, "*gens figés dans la paix des habitudes*," is admirably depicted. Mademoiselle Annette's uncle, the millionaire, Pierre Denys Nicollet, having heaped up wealth in America, returns to Bielle and attempts to transform it according to American ideas.

But Bielle, unlike Vallanches, clings to its primitive conditions, refuses to be Americanised, and in the end it is the millionaire who is converted. He is brought to reverence, as the two most important principles of life, the spirit of sacrifice which he discerns in his niece, and the spirit of primitive labour which he discovers in his brother, the gardener. He arrives at the conclusion that " simple and productive toil is infinitely superior to complicated, scientific, and lucrative work."

Both in *Là Haut* and *Mademoiselle Annette* it is obvious that economic problems have arrested the writer's attention. In *Un Vainqueur*, published in 1905, such a problem furnishes the chief interest of the story. The plot resolves itself into the duel between capital and labour, between employer and employed, between the middle class and the proletariat. The question is skilfully and impartially stated, but no solution is offered. "Perhaps we shall know some day" is the author's very vague conclusion. "The Conqueror," Alcide Délémont, who by the sweat of his brow has risen from the rank of employé to that of employer, is a fine figure, a very Hercules of industrialism willing to sacrifice himself, his family, and the human race, if needs be, to *Ce Moloch des affaires*. To him it is no matter whether the children employed in his workshops have or have not attained the legal age. His one concern is the prosperity of his factory, which needs children as well as coal, potassium, machinery, and men. This novel, in a *genre* quite different from the author's previous work, is as redolent of the atmosphere of the factory as those powerful scenes of *L'Assommoir* where the washerwoman meets her lover by his forge.

L'Indocile, Monsieur Rod's next novel, appeared a few months after *Le Vainqueur*, to which it may be regarded as the sequel, in that we meet with many of the same characters in the two books. But the world of *L'Indocile* and the problems with which it deals are not those of the preceding work.

To find a clear presentment of the various currents of French intellectual life at the present day, one cannot do better than turn to *L'Indocile.* There we have a trio of friends, Paris University students: one, Urbain, is a pronounced Radical, a self-confident optimist, who cries "look without," who believes that the world is to be saved and saved rapidly by acts of parliament; another, Claude, is a fervent Catholic, who cries "look within," his only hope for mankind is in the changing of men's hearts; and, holding the balance between these two opposite poles of thought, stands the third friend, an anarchic individualist, Valentin, l' Indocile.

Agnostic as he is, Monsieur Rod does not hesitate to expose the narrowness of the new secular religion which is growing up in France.

It has become a commonplace to say that in France, the country which has adopted the word *Liberté* as her motto, the true meaning of the term is unknown. "Liberty is to walk straight, to think rightly! No one has the liberty to fall into error or superstition," remarks one of the characters in this book; and such is the opinion of most intellectual Frenchmen to-day. Indeed, as Monsieur Rod powerfully points out, this new secular religion is as intolerant as the old Church.

"Now it is our turn to excommunicate," cries the rich anti-clerical wine merchant in *L'Indocile.* "We will excommunicate the Pope! the Monks! the Priests!" Valentin, who holds himself aloof from all parties, hearing such language, remarks truly: "I see the dawn of a new religion, new idols, a new gospel, a new fanaticism."

Readers of Anatole France's *Sur la Pierre Blanche* will remember that in the last chapter of that book, where he anticipates the world in 2270, in a deeply significant passage he foretells the destruction of liberty. "Society cannot permit liberty, since there is none in nature," he writes. "There is no being in existence that is free. Formerly it was said that a man was free when he merely obeyed laws. That was puerile."

L'Indocile reveals the writer's wise comprehension of the significance of events and keen insight into the character of the young Frenchman of to-day. He sees clearly whither things are tending in France. He portrays admirably that temperament dominated by abstract logic which is much more common among Latin races than in our own country. In the phase of development his talent has reached, the interest of his novels is infinitely broader than in his earlier works.

In a novel with the title *L'Incendie*, published in 1906, he reverts to the earlier theme of Swiss peasant life. The plot recalls that of a previous tale, *L'Eau Courante*. In both novels the story is of those who vainly contend with rapidly approaching economic disaster. In *L'Incendie* the prevailing tone is a little less dark than in the earlier work. Our author recognises that good does exist side by side with evil; and we are grateful to him for painting as the closing scene a picture in which loving-kindness predominates.

Monsieur Rod's last book, *L'Ombre qui s'etend sur la Montagne*, which appeared in the March of 1907, is a novel of passion. Here he deals with the problem treated seven years earlier in *Au Milieu du Chemin*. In both novels we have the waves of passion dashing against the barriers of conventional law, and ending not in the complete shipwreck of *Le Dernier Refuge*, the most pessimistic of all his writings, but in the sacrifice of the individual to society. Here, as elsewhere, it is the woman who makes the sacrifice.

Rather than break up her home and darken her daughter's life, Irène Jaffé parts from Lysel, whom for years she has loved with an ardent passion, strictly controlled within Platonic bounds. It is the old theme of the conflict between love and duty. Irène deciding in favour of duty, sacrifices her happiness. As the shadows fall upon the mountains, so does the sun fade from Irène's life. Death mercifully intervenes to end her joylessness. At the last her husband relents and summons the lover to Irène's death-bed. In the contemplation of the woman's unselfishness the two men are reconciled. "It was not to please herself that she stayed by my fireside," says the husband. "Neither was it through self-love that she gave her heart to me," says the lover.

Such a romantic conclusion is unsatisfactory from a realistic point of view; and the book would have done better to end with Irène's renunciation of her lover. Yet the volume as a whole, although less powerful than its prototype, *Au Milieu du Chemin*, is deeply interesting.

Increasing years and family ties transform the principles of husband and wife, while upon the lover they leave no imprint. Franz Lysel retains all the buoyancy and ardour of youth. A great musician, he is a typical artist, a Polish exile, without home or country. For him love is everything. His is an attractive child-like nature, ever young, impetuous, and irreflective, without guile and without malice. When Irène breaks with him, his love remains unchanged and reveals no bitterness. The husband, Monsieur Jaffé, in spite of a calm philosophical temperament, had in his youth held views so thoroughly individualist as to border on anarchy. He and his wife, when they married, had resolved that if ever weighty reasons should make them desire to separate, neither would raise any obstacle to the other's taking such a step; and they had gone so far as each to sign a paper to that effect. But, as the years drag on, and as their child grows up, although affinity between them has long since vanished, and although the husband is aware of his wife's attachment to Lysel, he allows things to remain as they are. Meanwhile, his philosophic studies are leading him from individualism to collectivism. He is arriving at the conclusion that "principles of the common moral code, arbitrary as they appear to us, repose nevertheless upon a minute knowledge of the sequence of causes and effects in the life of individuals and in that of the race." At the same time his daughter is growing obviously observant and critical of her parents' disunion and its chief cause. New influences bring Monsieur Jaffé to put that alternative before his wife, which results in her separation from her lover. For she has almost unconsciously been treading the same path of intellectual experience as her husband; and, although at first she repels his suggestion, she is afterwards bound to admit, "I too have sometimes had those ideas."

Irène Jaffé is the typical Rod heroine. Her yearning for self-sacrifice is the undercurrent of her being. As years advance she passes from the passion of youth to the serene reflectiveness of middle age; she controls the impulse of her early ardour, and it is only for Lysel's sake, not for her own, that she hesitates at first to sacrifice her love and serve "the universal order."

The minor characters in the story, like the

protagonists, are well drawn, and have a strong grip on the memory. Madame Storm, Irène's mother, is a common butterfly type of person flitting from one fashionable resort to another, ever seeking pleasure and failing to find it. Anne Marie, the daughter, old for her years, is as grave and self-contained as her philosophic father. Hugo Meyer, the aged musician, and his companion Louise, stand out well, with strong individualities of their own.

Among the many beautiful descriptive passages of this work, the finest is the scene at the first night of Lysel's opera. Monsieur Rod, himself a musician, has in reality here written a symphony in words. The succeeding waves of emotion passing over the audience, changing from approval to censure; the loud applause of sincere delight yielding to that of mere courtesy, merging again into murmurs of discontent and finally culminating in a storm of howls and hisses, are depicted with striking skill. In the early chapters of the book, where the action is laid in that Alpine country the writer loves, there is fine word painting in the romantic scenes of the sunset upon the Jungfrau and the bright freshness of a summer morning in the gardens of Interlaken.

As in earlier novels, the changing landscape is intended to indicate the future vicissitudes in the lives of those who gaze upon it; the dark shadows stretching over the Jungfrau are the symbols of the coming sorrow which is to overcast the lives of Irène Jaffé and Franz Lysel.

In psychological insight and high moral tone this last production of our author's pen takes equal rank with his previous work. It is not by the grace of his style, nor by the artistic construction of his plots, nor by the subtlety of his wit that Monsieur Rod recommends himself to his readers. It is above all things by the high seriousness of his work. He remains a powerful portrayer of passion, a patient seeker after moral truth devoid of prejudice, generally sincere and frank. His novels are the faithful record of the evolution of a thoughtful mind; and as such, rather than as great artistic creations, they cannot fail to interest the serious reader.

PIERRE LOTI

THE WORKS OF PIERRE LOTI

1879. **Azyadé.**
1880. **Le Mariage de Loti.**
1881. **Le Roman d'un Spahi.**
1882. **Fleurs d'Ennui.**
Rarahu.
1883. **Mon Frère Yves.**
1884. **Les Trois Dames de Kasbah.**
1886. **Pêcheurs d'Islande.**
1887. **Propos d'Exil.**
Madame Chrysanthème.
1890. **Le Roman d'un Enfant.**
1891. **Le Livre de la Pitié et de la Mort.**
1892. Discours de Réception à l'Académie Française.
Fantôme d'Orient.
1893. **L'Exilée.**
1893. Japoneries d'Automne.
1895. Le Désert.
Jérusalem.
Galilée.
1897. **Ramuntcho.**
Figures et Choses qui passaient.
1898. Judith Renaudin. (Drama.)
1899. **Reflets sur la Sombre Route.**
1902. Les Derniers Jours de Pékin.
1903. L'Inde sans les Anglais.
1904. Vers Ispahan.
1905. **La Troisième Jeunesse de Madame Prune.**
1906. **Les Désenchantées.**
Translation of "King Lear."

PIERRE LOTI, 1850

" The most delicate visionary of our time, at once the most primitive and the most complex of beings, with the senses of a primitive savage . . . and a soul as decadent as the most decadent among moderns."—PAUL BOURGET.

THE works of no French writer are more widely read than those of Pierre Loti. In Turkish harems and London drawing-rooms they are equally popular. His novels have hardly appeared in Paris when they are translated into all European languages. Nevertheless Loti, one of the most successful of living writers, is not a novelist by profession. Like Joseph Conrad, whose works in some respects those of Loti resemble, he is a sailor. His first novel, *Azyadé*, published anonymously in 1879, was inspired by his travels. Its success attracted the attention of that brilliant woman of letters and of society, Madame Adam. Loti became an habitué of her salon and a writer in *La Nouvelle Revue*. From that moment his fortune as a writer was made. From that time down to the present he has continued to produce a series of works varying greatly in merit, but all bearing the impress of the true artist's touch. Many of them have appeared serially in the pages of *La Nouvelle Revue*.

"What women want in stories," said an eminent writer the other day, "is a good deal of love, a little murder, and the best of them some religion." Whether such a statement might not apply to a certain class of men readers as well as to women is a matter of opinion. It is certain, however, that, no matter to which sex they belong, such readers would not find satisfaction in the novels of Pierre Loti. The love interest in his books, with the exception of *Les Pêcheurs d'Islande*, is weak. Murder finds no place in his stories, and his pages express no deep religious feeling. Why, then, is Loti so widely read, not only in France, but throughout the world? Not certainly for the plots of his novels; they are always vague and sometimes quite untraceable. Not for his insight into character; he is no psychologist. Mr. Henry James is one of his most ardent admirers; but even he is forced to admit that Loti, "when he lays hands on the spirit of man, ceases to be expert." In what respect is he expert then, and why do we read him? Not for high moral teaching. Shelley says somewhere, "You might as well go to a gin palace for a leg of mutton as come to me for rules of conduct." The same is true of Loti. We must not expect to find in his novels that assertion of the spiritual as against the temporal which characterises some of the best French novels of the present day. Loti is "a mere sponge for the sensations," has been aptly said. He himself is perfectly candid on this point. In his first published work he makes his confession of faith, or rather his confession of *no* faith. "There is no God, there is no moral code," he writes, "nothing exists of all we have been taught to respect; while we wait for the final horror, death, it is reasonable that we should ask from fast fleeting life all it can give. The true evils of life are illness, ugliness, and old age; neither you nor I are attacked by them . . . therefore let us enjoy life. I will open my heart to you, I will make you my confession of faith. My rule of conduct is to do always what I like, in defiance of all moral laws and all social conventions. I do not believe in anything or anybody; I have no faith and no hope."

Again: why do we read Loti? After this brutal statement of sceptical egoism, you will probably reply: "We will not read Loti." Should you come to such a decision, however, you will lose a very real pleasure. It is vain to expect moral teaching in Loti's novels. Go to him for what he can give, and does give, superabundantly. Go to him for the perfection of spontaneous art, for the keenest sense of the beauty of the universe. He is, above all things, a word painter; *Un paysagiste sentimental* he has been truly called. He possesses that rare artistic faculty of observing himself, analysing his own emotions and crystallising his memories. As Mr. Henry James reminds us, "His art is to express the life, to picture the multitudinous experience of the senses. With the deeper, subtler inward life, the wonderful adventures of the soul he does not concern himself." Holiness has no attraction for him.

Through his love of art for art's sake, Loti might be classed with the realists of Flaubert's school. He is almost as great an artist in words as Flaubert himself. He is as much a realist as Balzac. In the mere animalism of *Les Trois Dames de Kasbah* he recalls Zola.

Like the brothers De Goncourt, he could depict in detail the death-bed scene of one who was very dear to him. And yet, although he has all these points in common with the realists, Loti is in truth no realist. There is a poetic glamour in all his writings very different from the dry light of nature which was the only inspiration of the realists. Loti is a painter; but he is also a poet—a poet in the sense of Coleridge, who opposes poetry, not to prose, but to science. In Loti's books, nature appears, not as she is seen in the light of common day, but as she is reflected in the mirror of the writer's own personality.

> "Oh, Lady! we receive but what we give,
> And in our life alone does nature live."

Loti is therefore no realist. To what school does he belong? is a question frequently asked. It occurs, indeed, in one of the writer's own early works, where his friend, Plunkett, receives the answer that Loti must stand alone, that he belongs to no school. But since then the term *impressionist* has been invented; it exactly describes Loti. His works are, indeed, nothing more or less than a series of impressions, often realistic to a certain extent, but glowing with a poetry and a pathos of which true realists know nothing. One of the most typical features of Loti's genius is what Sainte-Beuve has called "the gift of tears." It informs all his masterpieces, his short sketches, as well as his longer works. No melancholy is so bewitching, so divine as Loti's melancholy, not Byron's, or Chateaubriand's, or Lamartine's; and it is never far to seek in Loti's writings, for there—

> "Ay, in the very temple of Delight
> Veil'd Melancholy has her sovran shrine."

The spontaneity of Loti's art is one of its greatest charms; and here again he differs from the realists. He claims entire ignorance of book learning; and, indeed, his style is quite unconventional. He scorns grammatical rules; and it would be impossible to parse many of his sentences. They are mere jottings, often in the form of an ejaculation, but each one as a flash of light, conveying its own distinct impression. His vocabulary is of the simplest. He employs only the humblest words of daily use.

The birth, the childhood, and the upbringing of Loti explain much in his later development.

Julien Viaud, for Pierre Loti is merely a *nom de plume*, was born in 1850, not in Brittany, as one might expect from his sympathetic pictures of the Breton land, but at Rochefort in Saintonge. In his writings he frequently makes mention of his native sands and woods, "*Les bois de la Limoise en Saintonge.*" As we should expect from such an egoist as Loti, his novels abound in autobiographical touches. In *Le Roman d'un Enfant* and *Le Livre de la Pitié et de la Mort* he tells the story of his childhood. His parents were Protestants, and strictly religious. One chapter of *Le Roman d'un Enfant* describes his father conducting family prayers, and tells what a powerful hold the parable of the Wise and Foolish Virgins took upon his imagination. Loti was the third and youngest child of his parents. He had one brother and one sister. As the youngest of the family he was thoroughly spoilt; grandmothers and grandfathers, as well as numerous aunts and great aunts, united with his own father and mother and brother and sister in fostering that egoism which was to be a distinctive note of his writings. Loti was a dreamy child. When he was supposed to be preparing his lessons, he was thinking of distant lands and tropical seas; and, as we might expect, he never got on well at school. His attempts at composition were the despair of his masters. At eight years old, to the amusement of his parents, he announced his intention of becoming a pastor. At the same time he had an ardent longing for travel. Pictures of palm-trees and the very word "colony" were enough to make him wildly excited. He used to pity himself when he reflected that as a Protestant pastor he would be cut off from travel; and he seems to have enjoyed meditating on this future self-renunciation. His ancestors had been sailors. His grandfather fought at the battle of Trafalgar. The sea from his earliest years had filled him with a sense of awe and mystery. In one of the most poetical passages of *Le Roman d'un Enfant*, he describes his first sight of the sea. He had gone with his parents to a village on the coast of Saintonge. On his first arrival he had not been able to catch a glimpse of the ocean, hidden behind sand-hills. But, as soon as dinner was over, he could contain his curiosity no longer. He escaped alone, and in the darkening twilight made his way down a winding path through the sand-hills to the shore. There was a keenness and a bitterness in the air he had never before experienced. He heard in the distance a dull sound, at once loud and indistinct. Suddenly there opened out before his gaze the ocean wrapped in the gloom of the evening sky. Paralysed by fear he stood still, while this dark roaring mass seemed to come up from all directions. Of a dark green colour, almost black it appeared, unstable, perfidious, engulfing. It looked malicious and sinister, while overhead the monotonous heavens stretched their mantle of dull grey. In this spirit Loti always writes of the ocean. The sea attracts him, and yet he mistrusts and fears it. "I had a presentiment that one day the sea would take me. I felt in its presence not fear merely but a nameless sadness, an impression of solitude, of abandonment, of exile."

"Thus *I and the ocean* remained face to face." Here is that arrogant note which is one of the greatest blemishes of his writings. Mr. Henry James endeavours to excuse this characteristic of our author by suggesting that other writers merely conceal their arrogance because they are afraid of appearing ridiculous, and that Loti cannot be blamed for not being possessed by any such fear: he is merely more natural, not more self-assertive, than his fellows. However that may be, one cannot help feeling that the introduction of his own personality in the face of the most overwhelming and awe-inspiring manifestations of nature is an error in taste and ridiculous. Victor Hugo was likewise a great egoist, but there is no such jarring note in his famous lines:—

> "J'étais seul près des flots, par une nuit d'étoiles.
> Pas un nuage aux cieux, sur les mers pas de voiles.
> Mes yeux plongeaient plus loin que le monde réel.
> Et les bois, et les monts, et toute la nature,
> Semblaient interroger dans un confus murmure
> Les flots des mers, les feux du ciel."

Loti's first experience of a sea storm was a great event in his life, its impression was to remain fixed on his memory; and in one of his recent writings, *Reflets sur la Sombre Route*, he thus describes it:—

"That memorable tempest of October 1859, the first my eyes ever saw and my ears ever heard . . . what I remember most vividly is this grey picture: One evening, in a terrible twilight, some big person, I do not know who, held me in a fold of his cloak, and, to avoid being carried away by the wind, sheltered with me behind a wall, trying to gaze out on the immensity; I, too, blinded, choked by the beating in my face and the stifling in my breast, tried to look; and a great music, as if from hell, rocked me in a kind of stupor. Near us were two women of the coast sheltering under the same wall, tightly clinging to each other, and trying to hold their cloaks, which, in spite of their efforts, the wind inflated constantly and flapped with a sound like the cracking of a whip; they also, like us, tried to cast sidelong glances at the terror, and one of them uttered hoarse groans, which were heard in spite of the wind." It interested Loti in later life to discover that Michelet was not far away watching that same storm, which he has described in *La Mer*.

Possessed by an ardent longing to penetrate into the unknown world of waters and of travel, it is not surprising that, in order to become a sailor, Loti should have abandoned his early stern resolve to enter on an ecclesiastical career. He joined the French navy; and by the time he was twenty-nine he had travelled all over the globe.

Then he appeared before the public in a new rôle, for he published his first novel,

Azyadé. Here Loti followed in the footsteps of Chateaubriand and dealt with the theme of "exotic love." *Azyadé* was followed by *Le Mariage de Loti*, *Le Roman d'un Spahi*, and *Madame Chrysanthème*, which are all on the same subject.

Loti, or a character whose fictitious personality thinly veils that of Loti, a naval officer, or in one case a soldier, voyaging from land to land and port to port, here enters into a series of morganatic marriages with the native women of the countries he visits.

The heroines of the first three of these novels: Azyadé, a woman of a Turkish harem, Rarahu, a Maori maiden, and Fatou Gaye, an African slave girl, are savages: "*de vrais sauvages et qui sentent la bête*," writes a French critic. In a later novel Loti visits Japan, where, at the port of Nagasaki, he takes to himself a Japanese wife, Madame Chrysanthème, who gives her name to the book. Madame Chrysanthème presents a strong contrast to the savage women of the earlier novels. Her mincing manner and cringing politeness make her appear civilised; but in reality her civilisation is only skin deep; it very imperfectly conceals a nature as essentially barbaric as that of Rarahu or Fatou Gaye. Loti's characters, both men and women, are always primitive creatures, if not actual barbarians; the weakness of his psychology renders him incapable of dealing with the complex natures of modern civilisation. In the first three of his novels the representations of primitive passions and impulses in all their simplicity is very powerful. *Le Mariage de Loti* is one of the most pathetic of his works. Loti and Rarahu are in love, but they do not understand one another. That gulf, in our author's opinion impassable, which separates the dark and the white races, renders any communion of thought impossible between them.

"What are you thinking of, Loti?" asks Rarahu.

"Of many things which you cannot understand," he replied. . . .

"Our race," says Rarahu, "differs so widely from yours, that whatever our missionaries may say, I fear that your God may not have come to save us."

Of such profound reflections Loti's Japanese wife, Madame Chrysanthème, is utterly incapable. She is a heartless little creature, whose only love is a love of money.

Loti has no high opinion of the Japanese. For him they are merely the oddest of marionettes living in paper houses, moving in a toy world of Japanese lanterns, dwarfed trees, and tinkling mandolines. Whether these toys have a heart or a soul is nothing to him. He deals only with external impressions, as in the opening pages of *Madame Chrysanthème* he frankly admits: "In the place of intrigues and tragedy," he writes, "I should like to introduce into this book something of the sweet perfume of the gardens which surround me, something of the soft warmth of the sun, something of the shade of those delightful trees. In the place of love, I would have you feel something of the calm repose of this remote suburb. I would have you listen to the sound of Chrysanthème's guitar, in which, as I have nothing better to do, I am beginning to discover a charm, in these beautiful summer evenings."

Madame Chrysanthème, in spite of her musical accomplishments, is incapable of inspiring him with the romantic affection he had felt for Azyadé and Rarahu. "*De cette Japonaise, je me soucie comme de rien*," he writes. What Loti admires in the Japanese is their artistic skill, their sense of form and colour, which finds such delightful expression in the severely simple decoration of their houses, where there is always a sense of space; how different, he reflects, from that so-called Japanese style in Europe, which consists in crowding together pell-mell ornaments and curiosities in a manner to give a real Japanese the horrors! The politeness and apparent amiability of the Japanese do not appeal to Loti. He mistrusts them, suspecting that they conceal a fundamental hatred of Europeans, which will some day declare itself unexpectedly. He believes in the Yellow Peril, and regards the Russo-Japanese War as its initial manifestation.

In a book published in 1905, *La Troisième Jeunesse de Madame Prune*, Loti returns to the scene of *Madame Chrysanthème*, as in *Fantôme d'Orient*, which had appeared in 1892, he had returned to the scene of Azyadé; but while in the sequel to the earlier novel he discovered that his old love had died of grief after his departure, in *La Troisième Jeunesse de Madame Prune* he finds Madame Chrysanthème characteristically cheerful as the wife of one of her countrymen.

It is interesting to note how the Orientals themselves regard Loti's descriptions of Japan.

A Chinaman writing in the *Japanese Mail* not long ago says: "If I were asked what book shows the lowest degree of European civilisation, I should not hesitate to name *Madame Chrysanthème*. To me the type of man represented by the author of this book is a demon incarnate." The Japanese also are deeply impressed by the callous tone of this novel, which, nevertheless, as a succession of pictures, is nearly perfect.

These novels also reveal Loti as essentially a Latin, always attracted by the people of the South, but utterly out of sympathy with the Northern races. He is hostile to England and America, indeed to the whole Anglo-Saxon race. During the Spanish-American War he journeyed to Spain to express, in a personal interview with the Queen Regent, his sympathy with the Spanish cause, and his dislike of the American shopkeepers: *ces commerçants d'Amérique*, as he calls them. It would be unjust to say that he is entirely ignorant of our politics or our literature. He has collaborated in a new translation of *King Lear*, recently acted in Paris. He dedicates his book, *L'Inde sans les Anglais*, to President Krüger, "joining his tribute," as he puts it, "to the immense and unanimous homage of all who in the present day have a heart, or even a conscience." In *La Troisième Jeunesse de Madame Prune* there is a passage of strikingly poetical description, but of the most arrogant and presumptuous egoism, where he describes the impressions produced upon him by the announcement of Queen Victoria's death. He is in his ship off the coast of Japan, when the funeral firing is heard. "*C'est la vieille couine qui est morte*," says his servant. "A grandmother full of days," reflected Loti, "has passed away over there in that island of fogs . . . no human being ever appealed to me less." In this strain he continues for several pages. As night approaches, on that memorable 17th January, the funeral firing, which has been going on all day, ceases, and Loti thus brings his meditations to an end. "An intense silence falls on this death : a page of history is turned : the proud old lady begins her eternal descent into peace perhaps, certainly into ashes and oblivion."

Perhaps there are some who will make bold to conjecture that the fame of Queen Victoria will endure almost as long as that of Pierre Loti. But we do not go to Loti for our international politics any more than for our morals. Did we do so, in his last book, *Les Désenchantées*, we should find ourselves joining Loti in prayer for the continuance and preservation of the Ottoman Empire and the Turkish people. "Religious and visionary, loyal and good, one of the noblest nations of the world, capable of terrible energy and sublime heroism on the field of battle when their faith or their country is at stake, may Allah defend you," he prays. In this novel the glorification of the Turkish nationality strikes a jarring note in days when newspaper correspondents are continually sending some new story of barbarism from the Sultan's dominions. Yet nowhere has Loti shown himself a greater master of style than in *Les Désenchantées.* His poetic descriptions of "the harmonious dwellings of old Turkey," of the wooded banks and blue waters of the Bosphorus, recall his pictures of the blue bay of Nagasaki overlooked by the spacious paper houses of Japan in *Madame Chrysanthème.* But in this last novel there is a deep human interest lacking in the story of Japan. The woman of the harem, Djénane, and her cousins Zeyneb and Otélek, with their minds broadened by western culture and their lives narrowed by Turkish barbarism, are infinitely more sympathetic than the heartless little Madame Chrysanthème. In all Loti's oriental books one is struck by the growing universality of western culture and customs, and the prevalence of that social mill in which—

> "We grind each other's angles down."

And yet, as Loti reminds us, beneath the veneer of occidental civilisation the oriental type persists. "*Dès qu'on gratte un peu le vernis, des petites barbares,*" says Djénane.

Many of Loti's novels are mere impressions of travel unconnected by any plot whatever. They are beautiful poetic pictures; but, like Lamartine's travels, they are marred by the constant appearance in the foreground of the more than lifesize figure of the author. The reader cannot fail to realise that the desert of Arabia, the capital of the Holy Land, the empire of India are merely described in order to form a picturesque background for the pose of the writer. When Loti describes in detail the Arab costume in which he crossed the desert, and the rich silks he wore on Mount Sinai, because they looked so well against the whitewashed walls of the monastery in which he was staying, the average reader hears a false note. Certain critics tell us that Loti introduces such passages because he is not thinking of the reader at all, but only of rendering completely and precisely his impression. But here, we contend, in the very fact that his impression includes such attitudinising, lies his weakness.

In his impressions of life, on the other hand, Loti is at his best. Perhaps the most deeply pathetic of all his writings is *Un Vieux* in *Propos d'Exil.* Un Vieux is an aged mariner, left stranded and alone in his old age, deprived of every solace and every joy, and yet clinging to life with an attachment growing stronger and stronger as death approaches, until his one aim comes to be the prolongation of his miserable existence. "But," writes Loti, rendering in a few graphic strokes a world of pathos, "one March night Death, passing by on his way to Brest to make an end of two or three consumptives, stopped and strangled him."

The same infinite pathos which is the note of *Un Vieux* is the greatest charm of Loti's two masterpieces, *Mon Frère Yves* and *Pêcheurs d'Islande.* These novels are much more than a mere succession of pictures. The first is the romance of a strong, helpful friendship between man and man; the second the simplest, deepest little story of love and death. Both are the expressions of the author's dominant passion, his love for the sea. In his dedication of *Mon Frère Yves* to his friend Alphonse Daudet, he says: "It was you who gave me the idea of writing the life of a sailor, and of putting into it the great monotony of the sea." Loti, however, does more than express "the great monotony of the sea" in these two novels. The ideas of cruelty and immensity are never absent from his conception of the ocean. The heroes of these books, the Breton sailors Yves, Yann Gaos, and Sylvestre Moan, are fine creatures, strong and handsome like the Vikings of old, with all the primitive impulses of those old warriors and sailors; at sea, heroes in courage and prowess; on land, children in waywardness and simplicity. But there is ever waiting to devour their glorious manhood the sea, *la grande tueuse*, "the great slayer," at once the nurse and the destroyer of her sons.

Next to the sea and seafarers, Loti loves

most the peasant world of Brittany, which he describes with a master touch. "There is always a charming pity and a kind of filial passion in his phrase when it rests upon the people and things of his wind-swept, wave-washed Brittany," says Henry James. There are scenes in these novels worthy to be ranked in the very first class of peasant literature, full of the most perfect poetry, and often so pathetic that it is impossible to read them without tears.

Mon Frère Yves, great as it is, abounding in poetical descriptions of the sea, of peasant life in Brittany, and of human nature, ranks far below *Pêcheurs d'Islande.* While *Mon Frère Yves* is a series of slightly connected sketches, *Pêcheurs d'Islande* has a certain unity. It comes nearer having a well-constructed plot than any of Loti's novels. Its pictures of the sea and the sad Breton land are perfect, but there is also a strong human interest; the characters of *Pêcheurs d'Islande* live before us with an individuality much stronger than any other creations of our author. There are scenes in this novel, the pathos and power of which lie too deep for words. One can never forget the picture of the old grandmother Moan, summoned to the port, and, expecting to hear of the promotion of her grandson far away on the eastern seas, donning her best gown and going forth joyously, only to receive the stupefying announcement, brutally delivered, "*il est décédé*"; or the well-nigh silent betrothal of Yann and Gaud, their wedding rejoicings in the midst of the noise of the sea, moaning like an abandoned mistress—for in his early years Yann had declared that he would know no other bride—and then, after a few weeks of joy, their separation, and that other bridal of Yann when "la grande tueuse" claimed him as her own.

Pêcheurs d'Islande is indeed a prose epic of the sea. From beginning to end old Ocean is personified; he is one of the living characters of the book. Here the sea has a unity of its own. It is neither a world of waters nor an army of monsters as the landsman Dickens represents it in the famous storm of *David Copperfield*, but one Titanic being more formidable even than the Minotaur of Greek legend. For Loti, the sailor, the sea is a foe ever mighty and invincible. It remains always the great slayer. This conception of the sea, expressed with consummate art, is Loti's most striking contribution to literature. Had he never written another line, *Pêcheurs d'Islande* would in itself be sufficient to rank him high among writers of fiction.

THE END